The California G

❦ A Guide to the California
By Eugene R. H

Acknowledgments

No book is complete without thanking the people who helped you make it happen. The following were especially helpful, and I would like to specially thank:

JUDIE HOOD: Who taught me how to use a computer, typed all of the first drafts, and fixed the countless revisions I made over the months. I could not have done this without her.

JOETTE JUDKINS: She painstakingly edited what I thought was a readable book. If I'm considered an author, it's in part because of Joette.

BARRY SCHATZ: A true modern day explorer who helped locate and recover the lost Gold Rush era steamship Central America. He provided me with first-hand details about this amazing accomplishment.

JUDY DOYLE (& FAMILY): For allowing me to use her Great Grandfather's Gold Rush diary as a primary source.

CALIFORNIA STATE LIBRARY STAFF IN THE CALIFORNIA ROOM: They were incredibly helpful in setting me up with Gold Rush era photographs and made research very easy to do.

Everyone else who helped or inspired me as I struggled along with my first book.

This handbook was written and designed using a Macintosh LC. Primary software was Aldus PageMaker ® v. 4.01, and mechanical graphics were created with Claris MacDraw II ® v. 1.1

FreeWheel

Publications

ISBN 0 - 9634197-1- 4 First Edition

TABLE of CONTENTS

✳✳✳✳✳✳✳✳✳✳✳✳✳✳✳✳✳✳✳✳✳✳✳✳✳✳✳✳✳

PREFACE

The California Gold Rush would have been an interesting time period to have lived. Even with our modern accommodations, given the opportunity many of us would gladly go back in time to share in the dangerous excitement of crossing an unspoiled continent, with the possibility of finding a fortune at the journey's end. It was the lottery of the 19th Century, and thousands were caught up in the intensity of the moment that really wasn't so long ago.

But the Gold Rush era was also a much more serious time. The United States underwent many transitions during the Western Expansion movement that even now are hard to grasp. During this period the Civil War tested our strength to stand as a nation, and its results are still shaping the character of this country. Advanced technologies we now take for granted such as communication and transportation methods were changing as well. They affect our current lives so frequently, we seldom reflect on the developments that have paved the way.

We can't know exactly what it was like to cross the continent in 1849, but we can retrace the trail and stop to visualize what it was like. Today we have to look beyond the modern highways, power lines, fences and convenience stores when we stand next to the places of history. Only then can we imagine the dusty faces of hopeful emigrants, sounds of bells ringing around the necks of oxen pulling wagons, and smells of crushed sage on the trail of a journey long since over. The obstacles and difficulties they encountered are not often thought about today. With the turn of a switch speeding along in our cars we can insulate ourselves from the simple discomfort of a hot summer day; an element that could not be shut out by the gold seekers as the inescapable mid-day heat struck their bodies and soaked into their leather soles and wooden heels as they walked. Technology has now changed that, isolating us from their experience.

Today the reality of a seemingly endless continent to explore or exploit is gone, and we have to face both the good and bad consequences of earlier actions and states of mind. To me, this is where the importance of history comes into play because we can not change the past, but we can remember it when we attempt to better our present condition. To understand the people of yesteryear, we must view them through the writings, photographs, objects, methods and locations that opens windows of their time. The story of the Gold Rush is one such marker of recorded events we can unfold to examine the many transformations that have influenced our contemporary world.

The Emigrant's Trail which departed from Missouri was the main artery of Western Expansion in the 1800's. Through Wyoming it broke off into several branches, some of which led to the California gold fields. Diaries, letters and newspapers of the time describe the people, landmarks and situations along this famous trail that reveal images of adventure, hardship and change. Using those sources, visiting many museums and spending countless hours in the field and libraries, I researched a modern journey tracing the land route to and throughout the Golden State creating an impression of what it was like. I hope that my view of the Gold Rush and descriptions of the sweeping changes that resulted will bring to life once again an amazing era that in one way or another touches us all.

✳✳✳✳✳✳✳✳✳✳✳✳✳✳✳✳✳✳✳✳✳✳✳✳✳✳✳✳✳

GOLD RUSH TIME LINE

1848 Gold is discovered at Sutter's Mill, Coloma, CA.

1849 **First wave of approximately 25,000 gold seekers reach CA.**

1850 Second massive migration of roughly 45,000 flood CA.

1854 **Sacramento is chosen as the state's capitol, and the largest mass of gold ever found in California weighs in at 195 pounds.**

1860's Hydraulic mining becomes widespread throughout the state.

1861 **The Pony Express ends its 19 month service as the telegraph connects the east and west coasts. The Civil War begins.**

1864 The main part of the Gold Rush is essentially over. The following year the War Between the States ends as well–President Lincoln will also die from an assassin's bullet.

1869 **The Central Pacific Railroad is completed linking the Atlantic and Pacific coasts.**

1870's The electric light bulb and telephone are developed and the technologies spread.

1884 **Hydraulic mining is limited by court order because of its widespread destructiveness.**

1890's Dredging is successfully introduced. This and large-scale hardrock mining continue to make significant profits in the gold fields.

1935 **Gold reaches a new high of $35 an ounce.**

1942 Due to WWII, the government orders all gold mining operations to stop.

1956 **The Empire, California's most productive underground mine, closes due to high production costs.**

1968 The last large-scale dredging operation stops due to high costs and environmental concerns.

1970's **The price of gold reaches an all time high of $800 an ounce. This stimulates new exploration and the reopening of some mines.**

1985 Modern-day treasure hunters locate a lost Gold Rush era steamship the *Central America* off South Carolina's Atlantic coast. It contained over three tons of gold in various forms.

WHY GOLD GOLD GOLD!

In the world we inhabit, just about anything in short supply is valuable, and gold is one of those things. It could be that rarity is the only reason we have decided gold is important, but it is also a truly amazing element. It does not rust and can be shaped into any imaginable creation. In fact, the metal can be hammered so incredibly tissue thin that some special candy companies actually cover chocolate with it. All of us have seen jewelry made from the yellow mineral, and many simply admire the emotional appeal of its natural beauty and sparkling gloss. But gold has also been important historically as well.

The treasure reaped from California during the prime of the Rush was vital to the development of our young republic. Since gold is a common worldwide monetary exchange, the United States Government has always used the metal to back up our currency guaranteeing its value. Bankers made fortunes buying gold from miners in the field for less than top dollar, and later resold it at higher prices sweeping healthy profits. On the other hand, they made money available for personal loans and to industries who created new businesses and jobs resulting in widespread economic development. Investors on the east coast who supported expensive mining operations in the Golden State anxiously awaited shipments of heavy gold bars carried by steamships thrashing their way across the oceans. These ships brought the fruits of California's astonishing riches delivering the means for our growing nation to expand. Ever growing transportation routes such as railroads that linked the east and west coasts were also built with California's hidden wealth. Additionally, major

western cities such as Sacramento and San Francisco were constructed with materials purchased with gold. And not too long ago, coins were made from the precious element as well. That same gold even provided income for the North during the Civil War.

The overall impact of California's bounty taken during the Rush, worth over $25 billion today, clearly played a commanding historical role in the advancement of our country. If you think about it, without California's buried resource fewer ***emigrants** would have been prompted to move west as quickly, thus affecting the course and expansion of the United States.

*Bold face words throughout this book are defined in the glossary.

Unidentified Union Civil War soldier from Ohio
(author's collection)

2

It should be remembered, however, that there were natives living in California long before any Whites, Latinos, Chinese or Blacks came to this land. The first people initially did not understand the effects these new settlers would have, nor could the natives realize that their traditional hunting and gathering grounds would be invaded by droves of gold seekers with ideas, diseases, weapons and values very different from their own. But with news of gold, the trails these first Americans traveled for thousands of years would be quickly crossed and overrun with people from all over the world seriously impacting their way of life forever.

Nevertheless, this is the way history was written in the long series of events that led to the expansion and development of the present day United States. The purpose of this book is to help you participate in understanding the people, places, **technologies**, conditions and changes that have made this chapter of American history so interesting.

SELF-TEST

1. Why is gold important to our society? _____
    _____

2. Why do you think gold is valuable? _____
    _____

3. List three ways gold is used: _____
    _____
    _____

4. Explain how California gold helped the growth of the United States: _____
    _____
    _____
    _____

5. Do you think the gold seekers understood the impact they would have on the natives way of life? _____ Why? _____
    _____
    _____
    _____
    _____

THE FIRST PEOPLE OF CALIFORNIA

The first inhabitants who made North America their home arrived thousands of years ago developing cultures and values independent from the rest of the world. Before explorers came, there were about a hundred different Native American tribes living throughout California scattered from the Pacific Coast to the Sierra Nevada Mountains. All made use of the natural resources they needed and did little to reshape the land. But what happened to them?

When the Europeans made their permanent appearance in California during the late 1700's, they brought Christianity, disease and the violence of a conquering people. Over the next century this would lead to lasting changes and destruction of untold multitudes of natives. By the 1800's only the remoteness of some Sierran tribes kept them protected from outside influences where their cultures remained undisturbed until the invasion of thousands gold seekers who could not be avoided.

California's original landscapes must have been fantastic sights to behold, and the earliest residents generally treated them with privilege, living in a steady balance with nature and each other. probably the most beautiful location where the natives gathered is what we now call Yosemite Valley. The

Yosemite Valley today as seen from Tunnel View

Indians named this same canyon "Ah-wah-nee" which means "place of the gaping mouth," and its mixture of various tribes became known as the Ahwahneechee.

Ahwahnee is a breathtaking valley shaped by the powerful forces of glacial ice that melted leaving behind massive rocky cliffs and waterfalls thousands of feet high. With time, this natural hollow of purity cut through by the Merced River eventually supported thick meadows and a variety of plants and animals. This completed the scenery in an unmatched paradise. Believing their gods had created this special place, Native Americans made this basin their home. Here they fished for trout, hunted

4

deer and small game, and gathered roots. Abundant oak trees supplied the nut meat of acorns providing a main part of their diets and a reserve of food needed to get them through the winter. The cycle between people and nature prevailed year after year, and the Ahwahneechee had no reason to imagine that it would ever end.

This life-style continued uninterrupted until sometime around 1800 when a disease drove the natives from their unspoiled valley. It was remembered as a "black sickness" and was probably a plague. Many deaths resulted, and the survivors must have reluctantly carried their possessions out of the valley to live among neighboring tribes. The "gaping mouth" would be uninhabited for a period of time, but its memory was retained through stories told during the long evenings of summer nights.

Almost twenty years passed before a chief of the Miwok tribe named Tenaya returned to Ahwahnee with about two-hundred of his people. For a time things went on as they once had in this lush, green valley of their old home. But by 1850 the foothills were filled with swarms of fortune hunters bringing their prejudices about Indians and the use of the land as well as diseases and unknown technologies. This was a recipe for disaster that caused the two very different cultures to clash.

The gold and new people it attracted made contacts with the natives unavoidable, but all encounters were not necessarily harmful. Some Indians who met miners on friendly terms often traded with the strange looking bearded settlers learning their unfamiliar ways and of the interesting objects they possessed. One newcomer by the name of James Savage set up trading posts and created his own uneasy way of living among the Indians. In order to establish friendly ties, he learned the languages of various tribes and took five wives! Even so, two of his outposts were attacked and destroyed.

The Ahwahneechee resisted the endless intrusion of the unwelcome outsiders who caused rapid change. They participated in killing raids on settlers, then retreated back to the protective rock walls of Ahwahnee that remained mysteriously hidden from the miners. The settlers who made little effort to understand the natives came to know them as "Yosemites" a probable mispronouncing of the word "Uzumaiti" meaning "grizzly bear," a symbol of the Ahwahneechee.

Also adding to the tensions, various tribes took advantage of the opportunity to hunt miners' horses and mules that were easy targets for food. The strain between the cultures worsened as nervous gold seekers who made no distinction among the different villages and tribes tended to shoot any Indian on sight. This propelled the cycle of terror and revenge. The official government policy was that all Indians who didn't adapt to the newly imposed society were to be either moved to reservations or eliminated, an attitude that was the beginning of the end for these first people.

Encouraged by miners who wanted their lives and claims safeguarded, government officials were soon called in to make peace. Their failure to settle the dispute led to the organization of a small volunteer army in the winter of 1851. Known as the Mariposa Battalion, its members chose James Savage as their "Major" who would lead them on a journey to enforce the "official policy" of protecting the interests ... ...e Southern **Mother Lode**.

...days of the Battalion's advance, Savage sent an Indian messenger ...o relocate his people in a peaceful manner. Concluding that he ...gainst the numbers and guns of the angry militia, the chief agreed ...e to a Central Valley reservation. But in the days that followed, the ...rised to find out just how few Indians were relocating to the arranged ...ing this was the entire tribe, the cautious army was led through deep ...to the upper rim of the gaping mouth where they first set eyes on the ...en canyon of Ahwahnee. The secret of Tenaya's natural fortress was ...any of the remaining Ahwahneechee scattered as the intruders ...last stronghold.

...y all in the Mariposa Battalion must have been impressed by the beauty of the vertical cliffs and waterfalls that had been concealed from them for so long. But as they explored these wonders they also made sure to destroy the Indian's winter food supply. Eventually, the new landlords renamed the canyon. Because most miners called the Ahwahneechee "Yosemites," it was suggested that the valley in which these Native Americans lived in for centuries be named after them. Ahwahnee has been known as Yosemite ever since 1851.

As for Tenaya, he was never able to regroup his people after the invasion and forced removal from his traditional home. He died about a year later while living among the Monos on the eastern side of the Sierra. A way of life had come to an end for these first people of California as it would for many other tribes in the coming years of the Gold Rush.

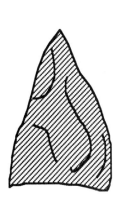

Self-Test: THE FIRST PEOPLE OF CALIFORNIA

1. Describe Ahwahnee: ______________________________

2. Who were the Ahwahneechee? ______________________________

3. What caused conflicts between the natives and miners? ______________________________

4. How did the Ahwahneechee become known as the Yosemites? ______________________________

5. In what ways did the Native American's way of life change forever with the arrival of new settlers from far away places? ______________________________

The properties of gold have been valued since the earliest of times. Egyptian and Greek civilizations were using it long before any explorers had reached the western hemisphere. In the Americas, the Incas and Aztecs built rich cultures around the precious metal. And while the natives of early California also knew of its existence, it wasn't a symbol of wealth nor was it important to their way of life.

By 1579 the English explorer Sir Francis Drake and his men anchored near San Francisco, what they called the New World, to make repairs on their ship. During their stay contact was made with the local natives, but they possessed no gold. Less than a year later Drake completed his voyage around the world and returned to Europe, but without the knowledge of California's treasure.

The Spanish, who had built a string of twenty-one missions along the California coast during the 1700's, never knew that about a hundred miles to the east, in the mountains they named, lay a fortune in gold. Mexicans living in Southern California found gold in 1775 while the American Revolution was being fought, but it wasn't enough to cause a major stir. By 1842, Francisco Lopez, owner of a large ranch near Los Angeles, again discovered gold. This led to a small rush, but it didn't catch on. As it so often happens, conditions had to be just right to trigger the events that would unfold the world's most famous gold rush.

In 1846 war broke out between the United States and Mexico. During the conflict, California was taken from Mexico by "American" settlers with the help of a small U.S. force led by Captain John C. Fremont. Since the army was not technically representing the United States, they could not raise the stars and stripes, so they made a new flag. Because of the crudely drawn bear it became known as the Bear Flag. When the war ended in 1848 California became a U.S. Territory, and gold was again rediscovered by a carpenter who was building a saw mill on the American River.

This time the world was ready. Word spread almost immediately that easy gold was to be found in California, but people far from the west didn't get too excited at first because communications were poor and transportation routes were not well established. Since few people lived in California, newspaper reports of abundant gold might only be rumors. In December 1848, the

CALIFORNIA REPUBLIC

The original Bear Flag was made from white cotton cloth with a four inch red stripe at the bottom. The star and bear were also red outlined in black ink.

hearsay was finally put to rest when a speech by President James K. Polk confirmed the dramatic truth. Thus in the spring of 1849, the largest single migration of people the world has ever known was on! Over 70,000 gold seeking hopefuls made the trip west during the first two years of the rush, and by 1850 the Bear Flag Republic became the nation's 31st state.

1. Name four early civilizations who used gold before Europeans explored the Americas: _____

   _____

   _____

2. Why didn't the Native Americans in California start a gold rush of their own?

   _____

   _____

3. What European explorer made contact with California natives, why did he stop here, and did he learn anything about gold? _____

   _____

   _____

   _____

4. How might U.S. history be different if the Spanish had discovered gold first?

   _____

   _____

   _____

5. Who was Francisco Lopez? _____

   _____

6. What was the Bear Flag Republic? _____

   _____

   _____

7. How was gold rediscovered in 1848 setting the Gold Rush in motion?

   _____

   _____

8. Why did it take more than a year for the rush to begin?_____

   _____

   _____

   _____

   _____

WHO WERE THE GOLD SEEKERS?

A gold seeker was anyone who decided to pack together the needed supplies for the journey and took to the road or sea. They were from all walks of life, but after a few months on the trail very few niceties separated the rich and poor, the educated and illiterate. Tattered clothes and bearded faces eventually became the universal attire of most. A large majority of these enthusiastic adventurers were citizens of the United States, but the Gold Rush attracted people from many other regions on the globe as well. **Ethnic groups** from all over the world were introduced to each others cultures, and beyond the common prejudices of the day, many friendships must have been made with open minds and common goals.

A majority of gold seekers traveled by land where they quickly realized the burdens of the trip and, upon arrival, the small, hard-earned rewards of working the gold fields. Most men expected to make their fortune and return home in a year or two. Unfortunately few ever became rich and had to be content with turning back safely to the comfort of their loved ones. Few women came to California at first because it was a difficult journey, and while the men were gone someone had to take care of the children, farms and businesses. It was women who were quick to fill this demanding role when their husbands came down with "gold fever."

By the early 1850's scores of women made the trek to the Golden State. Some came with husbands, others were looking for one; many wanted a new start in life. Countless others came as "ladies of the night." None the worse for wear after their long journey, they were a very welcome sight throughout Mother Lode towns, some of which had a ratio of one hundred lonely men to every available female. When women did arrive, they had a civilizing effect on the men. It wasn't long before homes, churches and schools began replacing the saloons and gambling halls that once took up the men's idle time. California was changing as a result of the variety of people attracted by the Gold Rush.

California State Library Archive

SELF-TEST: WHO WERE THE GOLD SEEKERS?

1. Where did the gold seekers come from? _____

    _____

    _____

2. Define ethnic group: _____

    _____

3. Why wasn't the journey to the gold fields what many expected? _____

    _____

    _____

    _____

4. What influence did women have when they came west to California? _____

    _____

    _____

    _____

    _____

5. Imagine you are a young man or woman preparing to set out for California in 1850. Write a short letter explaining your reasons for going west to those you are leaving behind.

DEAR _____ ,

_____

_____

_____

_____

_____

_____

_____

SIGNED, _____

CALIFORNIA GEOGRAPHY MAP "A"

MAP "A" Shows three geographical regions in California. Each area is marked with the first letter of its name. As you continue this guide, the places you learn about will be mentioned throughout the various passages you read. So be sure to remember the locations you study.

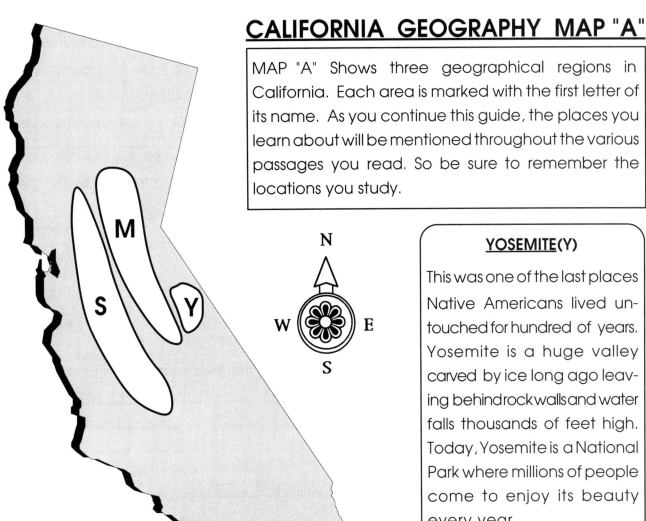

YOSEMITE(Y)

This was one of the last places Native Americans lived un-touched for hundred of years. Yosemite is a huge valley carved by ice long ago leaving behind rock walls and water falls thousands of feet high. Today, Yosemite is a National Park where millions of people come to enjoy its beauty every year.

Color Yosemite

[ ] **RED**

SAN JOAQUIN VALLEY(S)

This region is also called the Central Valley and is known throughout the world as a famous agricultural cen-ter. The land is flat and water is avail-able for irrigation making it perfect for farming. Many nuts, fruits and vegetables sold across the country are grown here.

Color the San Joaquin Valley

[ ] **GREEN**

MOTHER LODE(M)

This is where most of the gold was found during the Gold Rush. This region begins as foothills on its western slope and soon rises to the mountains named the Sierra Nevada. Many trees covered this area that supplied fuel and building materials for the thousands who settled in this unique beltway.

Color the Mother Lode

[ ] **YELLOW**

Throughout this guide the following geographical features will be mentioned so be sure to know their locations before continuing. A color key has been provided for you to complete and study before going to the self-test on the next page.

Pacific Ocean

Rivers

TRACE each river with a color of your choice as you follow its path.

☐ 1 SAN JOAQUIN   ☐ 5 AMERICAN

☐ 2 MERCED   ☐ 6 YUBA

☐ 3 TUOLUMNE   ☐ 7 FEATHER

☐ 4 STANISLAUS   ☐ 8 SACRAMENTO

☐ 9 MOKELUMNE

LAKE TAHOE (T)

This is the third deepest lake in the world with a depth of over 1600 feet. It was formed when an ancient volcano blew off its top and eventually filled with water. Many miners and loggers knew this famous lake during their stay.

☐ Color Lake Tahoe **BLUE**

GOOSE LAKE (G)

This body of water is a natural habitat for wildlife and was a familiar sight to many 49ers on the Lassen Trail as they rested before continuing on to the gold fields.

☐ Color Goose Lake **GREEN**

SAN FRANCISCO BAY (F)

This large natural bay is the west coast's most famous. Notice that all rivers eventually drain into San Francisco Bay. The Pacific entrance was known as the "Golden Gate" where many fortune seekers arrived by sea on their way to the gold fields. They continued their trip from here by foot, stage or steamboat to the city of Sacramento, which was a major jumping-off point to the mining camps.

☐ Color San Francisco Bay area **ORANGE**

MOUNTAIN RANGES

These two mountain ranges were the most familiar to the miners of the day. The Sierra Nevada to the east are rugged and were dangerous for the pioneers to cross – especially if caught in a snow storm. The Coastal Range, next to the Pacific Ocean, was not very hazardous, yet was a natural barrier that was passed by many travelers going to or leaving the gold fields. With colors of your choice, fill each mountain range symbol on the map.

△ SIERRA NEVADA MOUNTAINS

◯ PACIFIC COASTAL RANGE

Self-Test: CALIFORNIA GEOGRAPHY MAP"C"

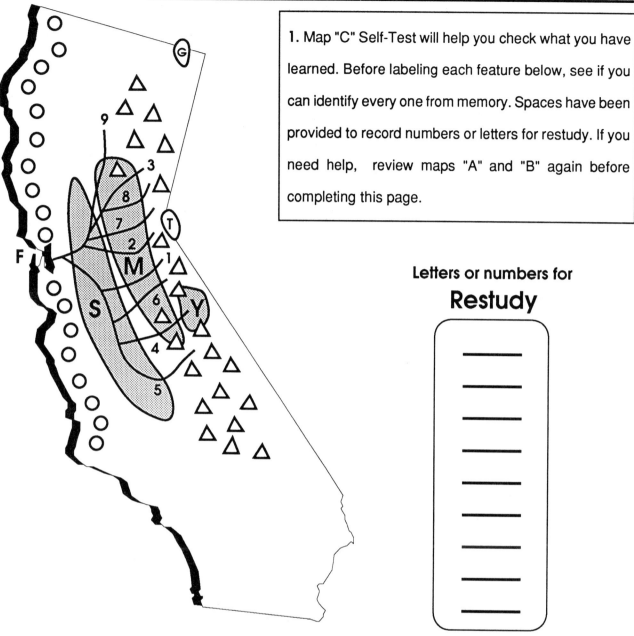

1. Map "C" Self-Test will help you check what you have learned. Before labeling each feature below, see if you can identify every one from memory. Spaces have been provided to record numbers or letters for restudy. If you need help, review maps "A" and "B" again before completing this page.

Letters or numbers for
Restudy

_____
_____
_____
_____
_____
_____
_____
_____
_____
_____

2. LABEL THE FOLLOWING GEOGRAPHICAL FEATURES
(River numbers on Map "C" are different from map "B")

Rivers

1. _____   7. _____
2. _____   8. _____
3. _____   9. _____
4. _____
5. _____
6. _____

Mountains

△ _____

◯ _____

Lakes/Bay

G _____
T _____
F _____

Regions

M _____
Y _____
S _____

TRANSPORTATION TO THE WEST

Developments in transportation from 1849 and over the next twenty years were dramatic. Although wagons and steamships were the only common forms of travel to the Pacific coast in the middle 1800's, many breakthroughs quickly followed. While thousands of wagons ambled west in the early days of the Gold Rush, they were unable to dependably carry heavy building materials and supplies in the quantities needed for California's ever growing population. Steamships were prompt to fill this gap as they reliably sailed into San Francisco's harbor with tons of cargo that could have not been delivered any other way. The drawback, however, was that it took months to complete a voyage that committed ships around the hazardous tip of South America.*

By the late 1850's western land routes were well established west of Missouri opening the way for towns. Heavily loaded freight wagons also began making regular but long awaited deliveries to the Pacific coast that competed with sailing vessels. Stagecoaches soon operated along these same routes condensing the 2000 mile, 180 day journey of 1849 into less than a month. That in itself was remarkable for the time, but in ten years there would be even more stirring change. By 1869 the United States had built a **transcontinental** railroad that spanned the nation shrinking the time it took to reach California to less than a week—an amazing accomplishment for the day. This progression of advances in transportation no doubt impressed travelers who had originally made the dangerous trip west, as developments continued to make travel easier and safer.

Cover illustration from a painting by M.F. Kotowski

*The Panama Canal would not be completed until 1914. North America's first transcontinental railroad was built across Panama in 1855 which helped eliminate the much longer Cape Horn route.

BY WAGON

Transportation by land in the early stages of the Gold Rush was limited to a small selection of boxy wagons, and the most heavy duty of all available styles was the German-designed Conestoga. At a length of fifteen feet, its large body was built with tall upward slanting ends to keep belongings from sliding out when navigating steep hills. Its rugged construction and large wheels made it very durable but heavy and expensive. Where smaller wagons struggled, the Conestoga's high axles made travelling over large rocks, tree stumps or washouts on the trail considerably easier to pass. Another benefit of this well-made rig was that it could be used as a boat when its wheels were removed providing an added option when crossing deep rivers. But even with the advantages the Conestoga offered, relatively few were outfitted for the long trip to the gold fields because the heavy loads they could carry were too burdensome for the animals.

Much more popular, however, were the standard farm or Murphys wagons that just about every man owned in the early years of agricultural America. These manageable vehicles were nine to twelve feet long, about four feet wide and much lighter. They were functional and affordably priced, but required modifications to prepare them for the constant abuse a journey to California would demand.

Called "prairie schooners," or ships of the land, all types of wagons had some features in common. Each was covered with a protective canvas top that was often treated with a sticky waterproofing mixture of beeswax and linseed oil which gave them a sandy brown color. The body was painted an eye-catching blue with red wheels, but even the cheerful colors couldn't hide the fact that every one had an uncomfortable ride. Because there was no suspension whatsoever, riding a team animal or more often walking was less tiring than a jolting wagon. It was recommended that no more than 2000 pounds of supplies should be carried on board for the four month journey to California; however, many were grossly weighted down beyond this. Each was pulled by an average team of four to six animals which would haul the necessary supplies for about five men on their journey west. With the above specifics in mind, it was generally only the driver, the very tired or the sick who rode inside the heavily loaded wagons.

A majority of people used this familiar method of transportation, steamships being the only other option, to reach the gold fields in 1849. It was geography that imposed the greatest limitations that extended the amount of time required to span the country. Nevertheless, land route technology was quick to lead the way shortening the time it took to cross the massive western expanse of the continent.

Wagon at Scotts Bluff, Nebraska "Tires" were smaller on the front to make steering easier

BY STEAMSHIP

If the geography of the land route seemed too frightening, a person had the money and trusted the experience of captains who sailed to the west coast, then transportation by steamship was the alternative. These sturdy work horses of the sea were equipped with sails to take advantage of the wind and save fuel, but progress was insured during stretches of calm or tossing storms with energy created by their coal or wood burning boilers. The steam these engines generated turned large side-mounted paddle wheels that provided dependable power to stay the course during the long journey to California.

These stable wooden ships were a hundred feet long or more and were usually filled to capacity with hopeful adventurers. The price of a ticket ranged anywhere from $100 for general passage to as much as $1000 for first class that included ice in drinks. Although voyage by sea could take the same amount of time as by wagon train, it was considered safer. The biggest challenge of traveling by steamship was to keep occupied during the long uneventful days on the ocean or conceal thoughts of terror during the occasional violent weather. In addition to carrying passengers, these steamships were a vital supply link in the early days of the Gold Rush. Since roads crossing the land east of the Missouri River were not yet reliable, these ships brought everything imaginable to San Francisco such as mail, lumber, bricks, tools, clothes, canned foods, mining supplies, stagecoaches, train engines and even a courthouse clock. Name it, and it was shipped to the west by sea.

Nearly 25,000 people elected to take the ocean route to California in the first two years of the Gold Rush. And even though nearly three out of four chose the land trails west, the return trip was quite different. Not wanting to suffer the hardships of overland travel again, eighty-percent of ordinarily luckless miners preferred the sea route from California via Mexico, Nicaragua or Panama. There was no shortage of ships in San Francisco Bay, and captains were happy to accommodate their passage. Steamships trailing their long plumes of thick black smoke would be very busy for many years to come.

California State Library Archive

BY STAGECOACH

By 1860 settlements throughout the west had taken hold and the stagecoach was a common sight making its way across the established roads of the plains, mountains and deserts of the west. Unlike prairie schooners, stagecoaches had suspension systems made of layers of thick leather that ran underneath the coach's wooden body supporting its weight. The ride was elastic, but compared to wagons it was luxury.

If fully loaded, the inside was cramped with nine passengers. There were six facing each other from the front and rear of the coach with three more sitting on the folding seat between the doors. In addition to the two drivers, three more passengers could sit in seats on the roof. Some luggage and freight went on the roof, too, but most of it was mounted on the back of the coach under a leather covering called a "boot" that kept off some of the dust. Travelers usually didn't arrive at their destinations very clean since a team of four to six horses kicked up a lot of dirt. At any rate, the speed of horses was often preferred over the durability of oxen and mules on the well established trails.

The cost to ride the stage west was about $300 from St. Joseph to Sacramento and lasted an average of 24 days. Relay stops were frequent to harness fresh horses, but after a long day on the road with knees jammed against those of another, it must have been a good feeling to know that there was at least the possibility of a soft bed and a hot meal each evening at the coach's home station.

BY RAILROAD

Railroads had been operating in the United States since the 1830's, and the need to build a railway connecting the east and west coasts was recognized in the early 1850's. But the amount of money, materials and men needed to accomplish such a task was almost unthinkable. Some thought the project would take thirty years to complete since the granite rock of the Sierra Nevada would have to be chiseled through on the Pacific side. While at the same time, workers from the east would face hostile Native Americans, namely the Plains Indians. They were angry about the ruthless invasion of their land and the white man's needless slaughter of the buffalo they depended on for survival. Many tribes sought to defend their way of life by attacking the whites.

Despite numerous problems, with the end of the Civil War in 1865, construction of a transcontinental railroad began to take place. Final Plans were drawn for this monumental task as two groups of workers were organized to lay tracks at opposite ends of the country. One outfit, the Central Pacific starting out from Sacramento, hired thousands of Chinese laborers who picked and blasted their way through the rugged mountains of the Sierra. The other group the Union Pacific hired many ex-soldiers and Irish immigrants who began to lay track a year later across the plains beginning from Omaha, Nebraska. Working at full speed, men on both teams labored exhausting one hundred hour weeks while earning $2.00 a day and living in mobile tent camps to complete the task at hand.

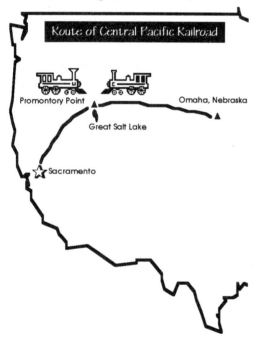

Meeting at Promontory Point   "Courtesy Union Pacific Railroad, Omaha, Nebraska"

On May 10, 1869 in less than four years, the two crews met and drove the last spikes at a place named Promontory Point on the north side of Utah's Great Salt Lake. In all, the Central Pacific laid 742 miles of track and the Union Pacific 1038. In the dedication ceremony that followed, two engines, one coming from the east and the other from the west, clanked noses as telegraph operators and photographers recorded the success of this impressive achievement. The Atlantic Ocean was now only one week's journey from the Pacific. In less than twenty years, a sometimes deadly course that once took four to six months of travel could now be safely measured in days.

The first engines to run on these tracks were noisy machines whose steam boilers were fed chunks of coal that belched out black smoke and water vapor through their funnels as they puffed along. At an average speed of twenty miles an hour, an engine pulled a series of comfortable wooden coaches equipped with beds, lighted by kerosene lamps and heated with pot-bellied stoves. General passengers paid $75 for a journey that left from Omaha, made nearly two-hundred stops for water and coal, and ended in Sacramento five days later. Troublesome as it may seem to us, railroads served their purpose; they bridged a nation at great speed, comfort and safety for the day. It would be many years before automobiles, then aircraft would make the next breakthroughs in transportation whisking us along even faster.

SELF-TEST

1. Explain how developments in transportation technology improved during the course of the Gold Rush and provide an example of how it continues today:

_____

_____

_____

_____

_____

_____

_____

_____

_____

_____

_____

_____

_____

_____

                                    continued next page

SELF-TEST: TRANSPORTATION TO THE WEST

Write a short description for the following methods of transportation including the advantages and disadvantages of each:

CONESTOGA WAGON

STANDARD WAGON

STEAMSHIP

STAGECOACH

RAILROAD

21

✠ TO THE CALIFORNIA GOLD FIELDS ✠

The smell of freshly crushed grass and earth filled the cool morning air as thousands of rattling wagons etched ruts into the rolling green vastness of the prairie. An endless blue sky highlighted the drama of the day in the spring of 1849 as mules and oxen bellowed out to their drivers, who were in turn shouting a variety of unique commands encouraging their teams to pull the heavily loaded rigs. A wagon stuck to the axle in a muddy bog from a rainstorm the night before was hardly noticed as company leaders rerouted their lineups on either side of the trail creating new ones. A dog chasing a small rodent bolted in between a wagon's iron-hooped, wooden wheels as a young woman walking with a friend commented that the eternal line of wagons looked like ships on an ocean of grass. Another emigrant riding his horse and fearful of Indians was checking the grease packed barrels of the ball and cap revolver he had recently purchased, as the smoke of thickly cut fried bacon from a late starter drifted in the air. While each day blended in with the next, so continued the epic journey of the gold seeking adventurers who became known as the 49ers.

DRAW YOUR OWN SCENE AS THE WAGONS ROLLED WEST ACROSS THE PRAIRIE

VOYAGE BY SEA

By early August 1848, news of gold in the American River had reached eastern cities in all thirty states. But more convincing evidence would need to be presented to the public to overcome the doubts of rumors and the expense and danger of an extended journey to California. The long awaited facts came in December from two sources: The United States Army and the President.

The military occupied California after the War with Mexico, and having firsthand accounts of gold strikes, sent to President Polk many ounces of the valuable metal to back their report. Therefore, the President spoke confidently with a single passing sentence during his State of the Union speech to Congress on December 5.

> **"The accounts of the abundance of gold in that territory are of such extraordinary character as would scarcely command belief were they not [supported] by authentic reports of officers in public service."**

With those fateful words and 230 ounces of gold on public display at the War Department Building in Washington, D.C., events began to take shape. Seemingly at once, every type of person ranging from farmers to city dwellers, preachers to businessmen, and the honest to the swindler all gathered their savings or sold everything they owned and set out to find their fortune. But first a choice of transportation had to be made . . . to go by land or sea?

If a gold seeker lived inland the decision was simple; he would take the land route. He probably already owned a wagon, animals and was knowledgeable with the ways of the land. Even if he was familiar with the realities of geography that lay ahead on the overland journey, the expense of a voyage by sea limited the option for many.

On the other hand, for those living closer to the Atlantic coast, the ocean route was the fastest way to the gold fields, and getting there quickly was important. Secondly, ships were available for transportation by east coast merchants and fishermen who sailed around South America's Cape Horn; they had earned a dependable reputation for making the 15,000 mile voyage to San Francisco. And unlike the overland route, where getting lost or failing to find water in time could end in disaster, ships were well prepared for just about everything except bad weather. These facts made voyage by ship a comforting preference for thousands of anxious gold seekers.*

Although the trip by sea was generally safer and often faster, it was costly. By the standards of the day, the fare for ocean passage was an average of nearly $500 compared to a price of about $200 by land. There were two main routes to California and by taking the shortest available line, a steamship could take an **argonaut** by way of Havana, Cuba

* Preview Voyage by Sea Map page 28 to become familiar with the locations you will be reading about before continuing.

enroute to Chagres, Panama. There he would leave the Atlantic side and cross the **isthmus** by canoe and mule train through dense jungle trails. He would reach Panama City on the Pacific side in about three days. From there, a northbound ship would speed him to his destination in San Francisco – total time, about six weeks. Unfortunately in 1849, the rainy passage across the isthmus had its problems with tropical diseases such as **malaria**. Another difficulty was a lack of regularly scheduled ships arriving in port on the western side of Panama; an unforeseen delay that could make this venture last more than twice its expected duration. In brief, the only way a traveler could guarantee his surest way to California was by taking the long route around the horn of South America on a supply ship. These passengers endured a trip that lasted anywhere from four to as many as six months depending on the varying conditions.

Three of the major U.S. harbors on the east and south coasts that departed with argonauts were in New York, Boston and New Orleans. A trip around the horn that began in mid-January would usually put a voyager in the diggings no later than May or June. There were two kinds of ships readied for the long journey. One style, known as a clipper, had a streamlined hull and was propelled by large wind sails. The other type called a steamer had a bulkier shape and could also be driven by the wind, but its source of power was insured with the authority of boilers if the winds ceased to blow.

THE BOSTON-BUILT CLIPPER SHIP "FLYING CLOUD," LOADING AT HER WHARF IN NEW YORK.

California State Library Archive

When a captain gave the order to pull anchor, say from New York, he could take advantage of the Atlantic tradewinds that would help guide his ship and crowded decks of passengers beyond the eastern edge of South America. Making their way into the hot temperatures past the equator, the next stop would be the city of Rio de Janeiro where they would arrive sometime in February. After resupplying the ship, passengers once again sailed with favorable conditions. As the voyagers made their way into the southern latitudes, however, the temperature became colder and the weather produced more rain, tossing seas and blinding fog. It was at this point the easterly winds could become less predictable and steam power would be an advantage to stay the course.

Although often sailing within sight of the coast, It would be many days before the travelers would set foot on land again. During this time the argonauts had to deal with long periods of boredom and the fearful possibility that their ship might strike a rock hidden by the fog or break up in a severe storm. As they steamed along, the cold days of the southern hemisphere caused the gold seekers to stay inside the holds of their ship. Many huddled around pot-bellied stoves passing their time by telling or listening to stories, perhaps while eating a meal of freshly killed boiled chicken purchased for the voyage. The dullness of the trip was occasionally broken up by fishing, shooting at bottles in the water, a fight brought on by confined conditions, or by some poor unfortunate who couldn't hold down his food because of sea-sickness; but seldom did the daily routine change.

The passing of the Falkland Islands during March signaled the next part of the journey. The waters of the South Atlantic were often violent, and the dangerous rocky currents of the Strait of Magellan were generally avoided in favor of a more southerly rounding of the continent's tip, Cape Horn. In choosing the safer route, the hazardous strait was bypassed leaving behind the ghosts of countless shipwrecks where less fortunate adventurers over the centuries lay forgotten in deep, icy grey water.

After rounding the horn at least 10 days would pass on the Pacific before the ship would anchor in the port of Valparaiso, Chili. Here solid land could once again be walked upon, and much needed supplies such as fresh meat, vegetables and water could be obtained while the ship's fuel bins were refilled. Taking a few days rest, the voyage continued toward harbors such as those in Callao, Peru or Panama City for one last resupply before reaching their final destination.

By April hot weather and generally favorable conditions began to replace the cold as they sailed on a northwesterly course toward Panama. Their arrival in Panama City was a big event for waiting argonauts who crossed the isthmus, because they were now assured passage to California. Farther north portages could be made at San Juan, Nicaragua or Acapulco, Mexico, but they were usually only visited if there was room to pick up more passengers. On the return trip, however, they were major supply stops and points of departure for those traveling by land east across Mexico to Veracruz, or to San Juan (North) on the Atlantic side of Nicaragua. But for now another twenty days would pass after leaving Panama before the fog of California's Golden Gate finally gave way to the land of their desire.

In anticipation of steaming into San Francisco Bay, passengers and crew alike crowded the decks to celebrate the end of their long voyage. Once the fog in the bay cleared, the appearance of countless ships became visible with their masts sticking up in the air like giant toothpicks on end. They filled every gap of San Francisco's harbor. Once their vessel anchored, the excited passengers frantically began their search for needed supplies and made arrangements to take a stagecoach or the next ferry steamer up the Sacramento or San Joaquin Rivers to the gold fields.

While in port, some captains found themselves deserted by their crews who caught gold fever and left with the passengers! Thus stranded, they became businessmen of a sort by selling sections of their worn sails as tents or renting their ships as warehouses, saloons, jails and hotels. In one case a ship was converted to a church. Since construction could not keep up with the demands of this ever-growing city, these captains were quick to take advantage of this profitable market. Business was booming in this once sleepy port town, and merchants of almost every kind soon realized that they had discovered the *real* gold mines.

San Francisco 1850, California State Library Archive

A fun book to read about travel by sea to the Gold Rush is titled: **By the Great Horn Spoon**, by Sid Fleischman. The book is fictional, but is based on many facts of the time.

SELF-TEST: VOYAGE BY SEA

1. Why didn't early newspaper reports convince most people in the eastern states there was really gold in California ? _____

   _____

2. What two things convinced people there truly was a gold rush? _____

   _____

   _____

3. Why did fewer people choose the sea route? _____

   _____

   a.   What were two advantages of the sea route compared to the land?

   _____

   _____

4. Why wasn't the route through Panama always the best choice ? _____

   _____

   _____

5. Why did many travelers choose the longer route around Cape Horn? _____

   _____

   _____

6. What were some of the problems aboard ship during the voyage?_____

   _____

   _____

7. How did some captains deal with their situations when their crews abandoned ship in San Francisco?_____

   _____

   _____

8. What do you think is meant by "Merchants were the ones who discovered the real gold mines"? _____

   _____

MAP ACTIVITY: Using the map on the next page, retrace the long and short routes described in Voyage by Sea from New York to San Francisco.

27   CONTINUED NEXT PAGE

MAP ACTIVITY: VOYAGE BY SEA TO CALIFORNIA

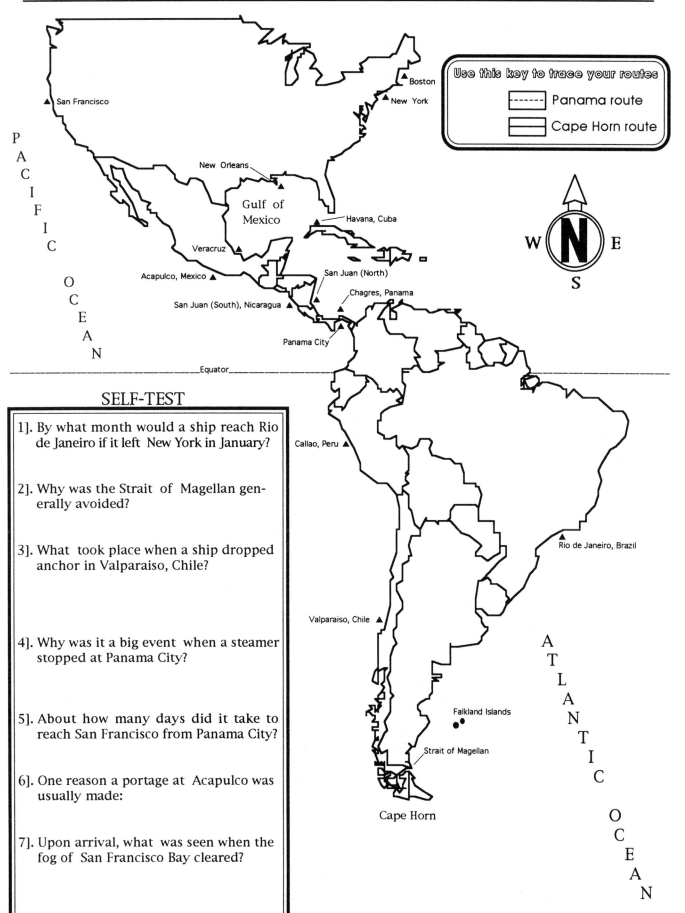

Use this key to trace your routes
- - - - - - Panama route
━━━━━━━ Cape Horn route

PACIFIC OCEAN

San Francisco ▲

Boston ▲
New York ▲

New Orleans
Gulf of Mexico

Havana, Cuba ▲

Veracruz ▲

Acapulco, Mexico ▲

San Juan (North)

Chagres, Panama ▲

San Juan (South), Nicaragua ▲

Panama City ▲

_____Equator_____

Callao, Peru ▲

Rio de Janeiro, Brazil ▲

Valparaiso, Chile ▲

ATLANTIC OCEAN

Falkland Islands ●●

Strait of Magellan

Cape Horn

SELF-TEST

1]. By what month would a ship reach Rio de Janeiro if it left New York in January?

2]. Why was the Strait of Magellan generally avoided?

3]. What took place when a ship dropped anchor in Valparaiso, Chile?

4]. Why was it a big event when a steamer stopped at Panama City?

5]. About how many days did it take to reach San Francisco from Panama City?

6]. One reason a portage at Acapulco was usually made:

7]. Upon arrival, what was seen when the fog of San Francisco Bay cleared?

JOURNEY BY LAND

The promise of gold was certainly strong to lure men into crossing the expanse of varied geography that separated them from the fortunes of their dreams. Yet for thousands of argonauts who chose the land route to California in 1849, thoughts of easy wealth would cloud over the reality of a long, difficult and deadly journey. Every type of landscape from boundless green prairies, swollen rivers, endless sage covered plains, hot deserts to steep mountains would first have to be crossed in order to reach the gold fields. Nevertheless, with gold beckoning on the western horizon, these adventurers were not clearly focused on just how demanding their trip would be. Rather, their thoughts were concentrated on what supplies and tools could be loaded onto the wagons they readied in anticipation of the earliest possible departure.

The 2000 mile journey across the continent usually began in April or May from one of two Missouri cities. Independence and St. Joseph were considered the last strongholds of civilization marking the boundary to the frontier and open west. These towns were full of activity with hundreds of anxious fortune seekers arriving daily by foot, wagons or steamboats. Businesses were selling every imaginable kind of need or want, and to be sure, the streets were filled with many people from far away places. With the exception of occasional accidents and deaths, especially from disease, that would shadow the men, women and children all the way to California, a scene of excitement and talk of hoped-for riches was everywhere.

Before setting out, many of the gold seekers organized themselves in the safety of groups. Known as companies, these partnerships were made up of anywhere from 2 upwards to 70 members. Collectively they pooled their funds to buy supplies and outfit the assembly of wagons and animals needed to haul their belongings. They agreed as well to share the necessary responsibilities this challenging trip demanded. Wagons were generally pulled by mules or oxen (same as cattle) which were more durable than horses under stressful conditions. Horses were also used but mainly by riders scouting paths or campsites ahead of the wagon train. Foods such as bacon, beans, flour and sugar were also purchased. These basic provisions would sustain them for the duration of their long journey. Once a company was ready to roll there was a choice of routes the 49ers could take west, but the Oregon-California Trail (also called the Emigrant's Trail) was the most popular because it was the fastest, most direct way to the gold fields.*

*Modern states will be used throughout this segment for clarity. Only unorganized territories existed west of Missouri at this time with the exception of Texas which became a state in1845. Trails had been opened to California and Oregon by the late 1830's, and stories of available farmland encouraged others to follow. In 1844 the first successful wagon train made it to California. See map on page 39 to preview the general land route before continuing.

*From St. Joseph, the heavily loaded wagons first had to traverse the Missouri River which would be one of many such crossings. There were no bridges built this far west at the time, so wagons were carried over for a fee on flat wooden boats called ferries. Most of the animals were simply tethered to the craft and swam across. Drownings were not uncommon, but once regrouped on the other side the companies rolled northwest through Kansas and Nebraska on a trail where few trees grew and the wide continuous grasslands of the prairie began. Since trees were scarce, the travelers used "**buffalo chips**" for fuel. Without natural cover they were always exposed to the frequent thunderstorms that prevailed in early spring, and their only protection from the elements was limited to their leaking wagons. The animals fared much worse, being completely in the open, they were sometimes pelted and injured by large hailstones.

"Tremendous Hailstorm" By J.G. Bruff 1849   Henry E. Huntington Library

As the long broken lines of wagons passed each other across the Nebraska prairie, deep scars were made in the confusion of trails. The companies were traveling through Indian territory and from time to time were watched with shock and wonder by Native Americans who called this land their own. But many of the gold seekers looking back saw only a threat and prepared for the worst. Indian attacks were not common, but the passing emigrants were still afraid and almost everyone carried a gun. In the evening, wagon trains sometimes formed a circle, but not because they were waiting for an assault as many commonly believe today. It was to made to form a temporary corral in order to keep their animals from wandering off in the night or being stolen. As the journey progressed, Indian attacks would be the least of their worries.

*Many companies used a guidebook written by Joseph E. Ware who had never made the actual trip west. Full of inaccuracies, he compiled known information about the trail, and made up other parts on hearsay. Attempting the journey himself in 1849, he became ill early on the trail and was deserted by his company where he died by the wayside several days later.

Eventually the prairie gave way to the gradually rising sage-covered plains that connected with the Platte River. This meandering length of muddy water would be a constant guide through Nebraska and Wyoming for hundreds of miles. It was at this point the appearance of backtrackers who had given up the journey were seen less frequently. It was also a time for raised spirits when natural landmarks such as Courthouse Rock, Chimney Rock and Scotts Bluff emerged in the distance as the emigrants checked their progression west. Spectacular stretches of scenery filled their eyes as the companies ventured far beyond any kind of familiar civilization until they reached United States military outposts. Fort Laramie in eastern Wyoming was one such welcomed encounter and provided the emigrants with an opportunity to send letters home, buy supplies and to rest under the security of the calvary.

Beyond the fort the companies continued to follow the Platte's westward lead. But after weeks of travel on this dependable water course it, too, came to an end. At this point they set out across an arid basin where they would connect with their next major water source, the Sweetwater River. It was along this river the recognizable feature of Independence Rock soon came into view. This large whale shaped feature was named so because many wagon trains made it to this point around the 4th

Emigrant's names etched in the granite of Independence Rock, Wyoming

of July. Thousands of 49ers camped here and etched their names in this large stone monument endorsing their advance. The journey thus far was generally routine other than passing the frequent graves of unfortunates who died in accidental shootings, wagon mishaps or even murders. But more commonly, diseases such as **cholera** took the heaviest toll on the emigrant's lives. Water was plentiful and fresh meat such as buffalo and antelope could be shot on the hoof. Travel across the plains in this unspoiled land was misleadingly easy up to this point, but that would rapidly begin to change.

This song summed up the feelings of many 49ers as they crossed the plains:

You calculate on sixty days to take you over the plains.

For there you'll lack for bread and meat for coffee and for brains.

Your sixty days are a hundred or more, your grub you've gotta divide.

*Your steers and mules are **alkalized**, so foot it you cannot ride.*

There's not a log to make a seat along the river Platte,

So when you eat you've gotta stand or sit down square and flat.

Its fun to cook with buffalo chips, take one that's newly born,

If I knew once what I know now, I'd have gone around the horn!

The companies continued on the Sweetwater throughout central Wyoming for much of July. Having had many days of good water and grass for the animals, the river was about to give way to the rise of the Rocky Mountains in the distance. South Pass was the access over the gradual hump of this towering barrier that separated the sources of east and west flowing rivers. It was not especially steep where they crossed, but the coarse, rugged trail, freezing nights and melting patches of snow that dotted the summits and valleys of this pine treed highland made their gain in elevation clear. They paid for this easy passage over the Continental Divide by exposing themselves to a shifting climate where thick, dark storm clouds gathered on the surrounding peaks. Changeable as the weather conditions could be, the companies would be changing, too, as they rattled across the landscape. Many companies which had once massed together now began to separate from each other as they gained altitude. Groups that had lightened their overloaded wagons earlier left behind companies who stubbornly held on to all of their possessions. But as team animals strained under the excessive weight, the decision to dump personal property became a necessity. The trail side was literally an open store with items such as storage trunks, saddles, tools, beds, furniture and even heavy iron stoves that were no longer considered important.

It was in the mountains that cholera mysteriously disappeared, probably because of cooler temperatures, but death for other various reasons was still commonplace. Grave markers were daily reminders of the danger along the trampled sage of the dusty road. But more immediate concerns would soon occupy their attention throughout this broad expansive plain filled with the bumpy ups and downs of ridges and canyons, spotted with alkalized springs and occasional rivers. The difficulty of travel continued to increase over the next variety of miles as the wagons pushed deeper into this unfamiliar continent.

Until now the emigrants had been traveling on the Oregon Trail. But not far from South Pass a decision had to be made; two routes parted which would both put the 49ers on their way to the gold fields. Taking one of the trails southwest would lead the wagons to the Mormon stronghold of Salt Lake City, Utah. Here the companies could comfortably rest and goods could be obtained. The disadvantages were that time would be lost and high prices would have to be paid for any provision. Additionally, the long, waterless alkali flats of the Great Salt Desert which lay west of the city would have to be crossed, and few considered this loop to be the best route to California in 1849. Most companies chose to stay north of the lake and progressed westerly on a faint path named Sublette's Cutoff – This led them to southern Idaho's *Steeple Rocks where they dipped southwest into Nevada.

Rough terrain and sometimes a confusion of untested trails challenged the will of the emigrants as they climbed and descended the mountain passes of the Rockies. The mules, oxen and horses of the wagon trains still had to be fed and watered which now became a problem. Most of the natural springs of popular campsites were already polluted by previous companies, grasses were all but gone, and everywhere was the debris of broken wagons, casks of spoiled meat, chains, washbowls and other assorted belongings.

*Today known as City of Rocks

Many times it would be necessary for a company to travel out of their way to find suitable water and grass. Tragically, a majority of the exhausted animals, struggling to pull their heavy loads and not getting enough to eat, slowly weakened. The trail was easy to follow for those farther behind as the bones of decaying animals and grave markers continued to trace nearly every mile to California.

By late June, the 49ers reached a last important lifeline on their journey. . . The Humbolt River Basin in Nevada. Temperatures easily passed one-hundred degrees in this wide, sage-speckled valley that was appealing contrasted by mountainous snow-capped peaks. Emigrants frequently complained about the poor quality of water, and the thin, flimsy firewood provided by the dense groves of willows along the Humbolt, but they also must have recognized how dependent they were on its gifts; passage would have been impossible without it.

As the companies advanced along the river's sandy trail, its powdery mixture of small, jagged pieces of abrasive rock methodically cut and split the animal's hooves causing them much discomfort. Adding to the misery of heat, loose sand and thick blinding dust, the Humbolt's many twists and turns forced routine detours away from the river which made travel extremely tiresome and frustrating. These conditions quickly took their toll on the gold seekers. At this stage tempers often flared, sometimes into deadly violence, but the argonauts dealt with their situation as best they could. All were inescapably bound to the Humbolt's harsh thread of life-giving water, and they would be for many days to come.

The emigrants travelled nearly 300 miles of this oasis-like waterway and watched it gradually become sluggish and narrower with each passing day. The river also became increasingly impregnated with concentrations of alkali which gave it a milky-green color and made it almost undrinkable. None of them had ever seen a river just disappear before, but like a cruel joke the Humbolt was, in fact, slowly draining onto the scorching desert sand and evaporating into a scum beneath the blazing sun.

Just when it seemed as though the companies were destined to push through more of this unmerciful territory, they arrived at a large area of patchy grasslands known as Lassen Meadow. This welcomed break came at a time when both men and animals alike were in sensible need of a few days rest before pushing on.

Discouraged at the likelihood of enduring an increasingly severe geography, many companies in 1849 decided to leave the Humbolt in favor of what they were mistakenly led to believe was a shortcut to California. By making this decision to take the route named the Applegate-Lassen Cutoff they hoped to make their journey less hazardous. Unknown to the emigrants, however, this northwesterly heading would take them toward obstacles that would make their course even more demanding and worse, longer. In the coming years this dangerous and lethal section would treacherously become known as the "Greenhorn" or "Death Trail."

Having covered some 1600 miles at an average of 15 a day, the elusive gold fields were still more than 350 unyielding miles away. It was now mid August, and a blistering hot, nearly waterless region beyond the Humbolt awaited the emigrants. The next 33 miles contained only two brackish springs, which were no more than small trickles that would supply thousands. They did, however, provide a means to survive as the wagons approached Nevada's Black Rock Desert.

The treeless, sun-drenched plain leading up and away from the river was a torturous stretch for the overworked animals which had been pushed to their limits in the searing heat. Many died or were dying along the miles of this mountainous pass by the time more fortunate companies had reached the second watering area named Rabbit Hole Springs. Even so, the several muddied pits dug out by the argonauts could not meet the needs of all animals and more slumped to their knees breathing heavily, eyes open wide with confusion, near death. Many companies were forced to reduce their loads yet again and had to combine their teams and supplies because of their loss. Abandoned wagons and valuable articles were everywhere, much of it burned or destroyed by its owners who were frustrated at their loss; they displayed their feelings of anger by insuring that no one else would be able to use it. After making camp around the stench of animal carcasses seething with maggots and buzzing flies, they filled their wooden casks with silty water and left this horrific scene with the morning light.

THE RABBIT-HOLE SPRINGS,

"Rabbit Hole Springs" By J.G. Bruff 1849   Henry E. Huntington Library

By noon the companies were descending the mountainous trail where they could look upon the level, white-hot crust of Black Rock Desert spanning nearly fifty miles across. Dust plumes choked the intensely hot air above the hard-baked surface as hundreds of wagons crunched over a basin of sagebrush leading to the barren reach of frost-colored alkali. Travel during the night was often preferred to escape the intolerable heat, and everyone able to walk did so to help ease the burden pulled by their thirsty animals whose mouths foamed under the stressful conditions. Everything was covered with a dirty, bitter tasting grit that even made breathing unpleasant. The temptation to save a few miles by taking an unknown path to the distant mountains could be fatal, so good judgement was essential.

The emigrants hurried across this indifferent landscape which took its toll on the sweaty animals who were allowed little rest. Mules or oxen that collapsed were prompted to stand and continue with calls and tugs by their drivers. When all else failed, they were often brutally whipped in order to shock the beast into carrying on. If this seemingly cruel last resort did not encourage the animal to move, the fading creature was unhitched from the wagon with the certainty that it would die. Their ruined bodies lay strewn all across this seemingly endless desert highway that led to the next available water 27 miles away. Grimly, their bloated, odorous corpses acted as quiet guideposts that kept wagons on course during the night. But it wasn't always dead animals or discarded property that marked the way. Occasionally the emigrant's were reminded of their own mortality when their lanterns illuminated human skeletal remains left by those without the energy nor desire to bury their companions.

Black Rock Desert in northwestern Nevada. The trail went by the dark peak in the foreground left of center where a hot boiling spring of sulphur tasting water (similar to the smell of rotton eggs) was available.

After several days of unforgiving travel since leaving the Humbolt, the companies finally made it to the next crucial water camp beyond this desert basin. There they saw the usual fallen beasts, array of wreckage and debris left behind to lighten the loads surviving animals had courageously pulled so far. Encircled by such visions, it must have been a strain to shut out this backdrop of scenery as they drank water or coffee, ate a meal of hard bread, beans, rice or maybe a rarer treat of sugar-sweetened dried apples or prunes.

The worst deserts were crossed by early September, and the emigrants knew the bulk of their journey was behind them. But in the distance beyond the miles of sagebrush, layers of a towering blue-grey skyline with hazy snow-capped peaks loomed clearer and more imposing with every sunrise. By now they had reached the eastern side of California, but imagine how weary these adventurers must have been. Many never got enough to eat; their clothes were tattered; their animals were haggard, and abused wagons needed repairs. To make things even more grievous after months of travel, a new disease called **scurvy** had become visible. Some no doubt questioned if the trip was indeed worth it at this point, even though it was unthinkable to turn back now.

Continuing on Lassen's Cutoff, the companies entered a pass near the Oregon border that led to Goose Lake where they stopped to recover. When they proceeded, the trail at last headed south into the heart of California. Travel through this region was exceptionally pleasant for a change as there was abundant grass for the animals, good water and plenty of wild game to be had supplying fresh meat. But as the 49ers made their way toward the Mother Lode, the trail again became more difficult with each passing day as they closed in on the high country of the Sierra Nevada.

As they approached the final mountainous spine that blocked their goal, the trail became threateningly steep, rocky and narrow as they gained altitude. Wagons could not even pass each other through most of this pine forested course, and once again the challenging conditions taxed the emigrant's resources. The sides of the trail were littered with the familiar sights of lifeless animals, smashed wheels, belongings and graves. These were the surroundings that tested their will; simply surviving was a real concern, and many companies broke up if they had not already. It was now late September and the fast changing weather at this elevation could easily shift from a soaking rain to freezing sleet or snow. Faced with the consequences of an unstable climate, an argonaut could be trapped and would be lucky to escape the Sierra with nothing more than what he could carry on his back or, more importantly, his life.

The final 35 miles of the route remained trying but finally ended at a settlement for which the cutoff had been named. Here the exhausted gold seekers could recover from their ordeal and make future plans. After the needed stopover at Peter Lassen's Ranch, necessary supplies were purchased here or if more convenient farther south at Sutter's Fort in Sacramento. With nearly six months of travel to their credit, the seasoned emigrants prepared for the reason they had come west. Rested and resupplied, the real search for gold began. (See Appendix A, Page 99)

SELF-TEST: *JOURNEY BY LAND*

A.   Name of an adventurer who traveled to California :   A __ __ __ __ __ __ T

B.   Groups of organized wagon trains called themselves a: _____

C.   Months the journey usually began: _____or _____

D.   One major city where the trail west departed: _____

E.   Name the first river crossed at the start of the route: _____

F.   Reason why the Oregon-California Trail was popularly used: _____

_____

G.   Animals generally chosen to pull wagons: _____ or _____

H.   Name for continuous grasslands on first leg of trip: _____

I.   Used for cooking fuel when there was no wood: _____

J.   Feared by the emigrants even though they caused little trouble: _____

K.   Major river flowing through Nebraska and Wyoming territories: _____

L.   Three natural landmarks that were passed: _____

M.   One reason military outposts were welcomed sights: _____

N.   Diseases that killed or weakened many travelers: _____ or _____

O.   Mountains entered through South Pass during the month of July: _____

P.   Three reasons animals were dying: _____

Q.   Why some emigrants went to Salt Lake City, Utah: _____

R.   Purpose wagons made a circle at night: _____

S.   Caused Humbolt River water to become undrinkable: _____

T.   Average number of miles traveled each day by most gold seekers: _____

U.   Name of largest desert crossed in northwestern Nevada: _____

V.   Foods eaten by many pioneers: _____

W.   Other names given to the dangerous Lassen Cutoff: _____

X.   Last mountains crossed to reach the gold fields: _____

Y.   Three reasons the final mountainous trail was difficult: _____

_____

Z.   Fort where goods could be purchased in Sacramento: _____

ACTIVITY: Write a diary for any three days of the six month journey as if you were there in 1849 after reading the self-test directions on page 39. Use the "diary boxes" provided on the next page or use your own paper to make it look "aged" following the additional instructions below.

MAKE YOUR DIARY LOOKED AGED:

A. Before you write, sponge very strong coffee or tea on your "diary pages."

B. While they are damp, tear off the outside edges creating a "ragged"
   look, then using a candle in a safe place, singe the edges.

C. When dry, complete your diary using black or brown ink to add realism.

continued next page

SELF-TEST: Having carefully read Journey by Land, use the map below to start from St. Joseph and connect, in order, the numbers and letters retracing the 2000 mile route followed by the emigrants to Lassen's Ranch in 1849. Also label **Famous Landmarks A through E** using the key below. Finally, complete the three blank diary boxes by choosing any of the seven numbers you linked that indicate various regions of the journey. Be sure to identify the month you would pass that area and include brief descriptions of things such as your company's condition, the landscape, climate or sights you would see.

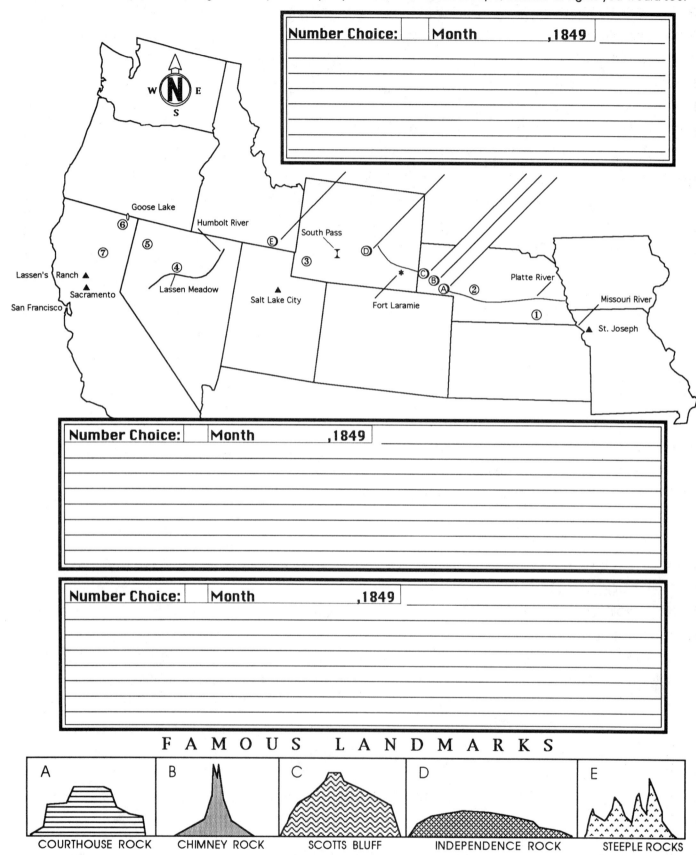

Number Choice: | **Month** ,1849 ___

Number Choice: | **Month** ,1849 ___

Number Choice: | **Month** ,1849 ___

Map labels: Goose Lake · Humbolt River · South Pass · Lassen's Ranch ▲ · Sacramento ▲ · San Francisco · Lassen Meadow · Salt Lake City ▲ · Fort Laramie · Platte River · Missouri River · St. Joseph ▲ · ⑥ ⑤ ④ ③ ⑦ ① ② Ⓐ Ⓑ Ⓒ Ⓓ Ⓔ

F A M O U S   L A N D M A R K S

A — COURTHOUSE ROCK
B — CHIMNEY ROCK
C — SCOTTS BLUFF
D — INDEPENDENCE ROCK
E — STEEPLE ROCKS

*Note: Modern states are marked for clarity since most of the west was unorganized territory at this time. Use an atlas to identify each state you would travel through on your journey.

WHERE GOLD IS FOUND

Gold is a very heavy mineral that weighs about 19 times more than an equal container of water. Since gold is heavy, it sinks and will rarely be found on top of a variety of lighter materials such as sand or gravel.

Bits and pieces of loose gold can be located in an assortment of places where water and gravity have deposited them, but the source of the element can usually be traced to a type of rock called **quartz**.

Over the years, miners have created all kinds of machines that make getting the metal easier, but no matter how hard they try, they never find it all.

For instance, a man who lives in the Mother Lode town of Mariposa was recently walking along a stream with his dog and discovered a two ounce nugget trapped between a split rock. The price of gold at the time was $350 an ounce. Needless to say, it was a great day for walking the dog!

work space

Beneath Sand Bars

High Water Line

Cracks in Rock

Between Rocks

Trapped in Grass Roots or Moss

Quartz Outcroppings

S T R E A M

—————— Self-Test ——————

After reading <u>Where Gold Is Found</u> and examining the drawing, list the six places it can be located then answer questions A and B.

1. _____   2. _____
3. _____   4. _____
5. _____   6. _____

A. Will gold nuggets ever be found on top of sand?_____ Why?_____
_____

B. If a gallon container of water weighs 8 pounds, how much would the same container of gold weigh?_____ (Hint multiply)

40

MINING TECHNIQUES

A variety of mining technologies were brought to the California gold fields as inventive fortune seekers arrived throughout the years. Each device attempted to make the separation of gravel and gold easier, but only the practical and effective designs survived the test of time. For example, one of the simplest methods, panning merely required a strong back and determination to slowly find one's fortune. While faster more efficient breakthroughs such as hydraulic mining or mechanical dredging turned out to be very effective but environmentally disastrous.

Although the prospectors of old were the first to sift through the untouched gold deposits of the Mother Lode, they never found it all. Modern gold seekers who use the same techniques of bygone days regularly wash out "color" into their pans and riffle bars. And as in the past, anyone who has ever uncovered a sparkling flake of gold shares a timeless thrill and common experience that has fueled countless dreams of hoped-for wealth hidden just beneath the surface.

Can you name the four mining techniques shown in this drawing and explain how each one worked? If not, read the following section on the various kinds of methods used to extract gold throughout the Gold Rush.

California State Library Archive

PANNING

Many techniques were employed to uncover gold, but panning was the most basic. All a prospector required was a pan, shovel, pick and knife to scrape out the places where gravity might have caused the precious metal to collect. Miners knew that **placer gold** was once naturally bonded within quartz and was loosened from its source by weathering or rushing water. Being heavy, the gold gathered under lighter gravels and cracks in bedrock when the force of water could no longer carry it.

To begin, a miner had to shovel deep into the bottom of a likely pocket of sandy gravel or scrape the contents of mud and roots from between rocks he picked apart. Adding water to the mixture in his rusted pan made it possible to swirl the contents around and around allowing the lighter materials to slosh out while the heavier gold remained at the bottom. As the assortment of sediments disappeared, a final delicate tilt of the pan's lip allowed the last bits of fine silt to spill over the edge leaving behind only black sand, gleaming flakes of yellow or maybe even a nugget.

The process of panning was tedious, strenuous and time consuming. Experienced prospectors mainly used this method in order to quickly survey an area before they staked a claim and set up more efficient equipment. Skill and patience would usually yield him at least $20 dollars a day from the icy water during the prime of the Gold Rush; but it was backbreaking work, and few ever made a fortune with a pan. Nonetheless, miners who exhaustively panned their hard-won profits sold their earnings to **assayers** who determined the gold's value and melted it down into bars for easy shipment. Applying a simple technique, these miners contributed to the incredible wealth taken from California.

California State Library Archive

ROCKER

A faster technique of sifting through gold-bearing gravels quickly caught on during the rush and could be seen along every stream in the Mother Lode. Known as the rocker or "cradle" since it resembled a baby's bed, it operated on the same principle as panning but provided miners with the advantage of being able to wash out more material in a day.

This process worked particularly well if two men cooperated. One would gather buckets of gravel while the other dumped the contents into a hopper that had holes punched in its thin metal bottom. Water was then poured on the material while a handle was rapidly shaken back and forth causing most of the mix to drop on an angled frame stretched over with canvas. Called an "apron," fine bits of gold would be trapped on the canvas while larger pieces slipped to the bottom of the rocker through a gap at the end of the frame. As the rocking continued, the water would flush the remaining material over a series of evenly spaced wooden barriers called "riffle bars". Lighter sands and gravels shook over the tops of the riffles while the heavier gold was trapped behind the bars where it would be collected several times a day.

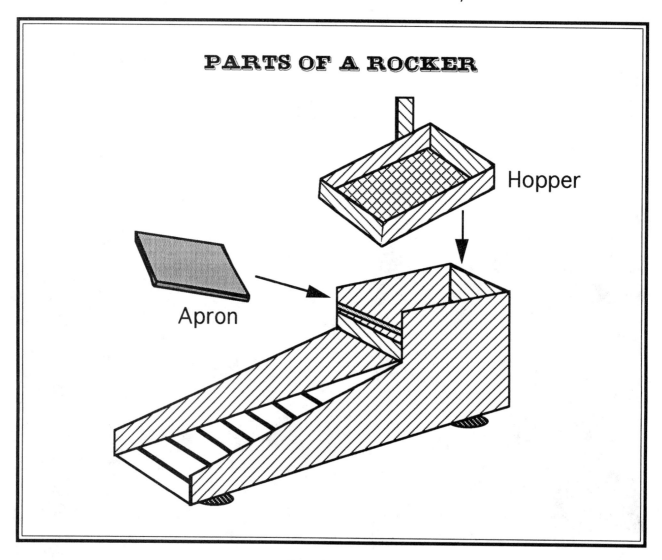

PARTS OF A ROCKER

Hopper

Apron

LONG TOM

There were other gold strikes in the United States before 1848 and one of the largest was in Georgia. When the rush began in California, experienced miners from that state brought with them their knowledge and techniques that made the task of harvesting gold even more effective.

The best known device these miners developed was called the long tom. It worked like a rocker except a constant flow of water diverted from a stream was channeled into a trough called a "tom." When miners scooped in the muddy sands and gravels they collected, the mix was agitated with their shovels. This caused the bits of gold and other materials to spill through half-inch holes drilled in a metal plate at the end of the tom named a "riddle." The filtered sediments then flowed over another trough containing riffle bars which trapped the brass-colored metal while allowing the water to carry away most other fragments of rock, sand and mud.

California State Library Archive

SLUICE BOX

Another mining improvement called the sluice box was brought to the foothills of the Sierra by the Brazilians of South America. In this method, an assembly of boards and riffle bars were nailed together forming a trough or **flume**. And like the long tom, a continuous flow of water was directed into the sluice allowing it to tumble over the series of riffles. Often long sections of these boxes were connected together so a team of miners working side by side could shovel a huge volume of gravel into the current of their man-made channel. By working together, they increased their odds of making this type of placer mining very profitable.

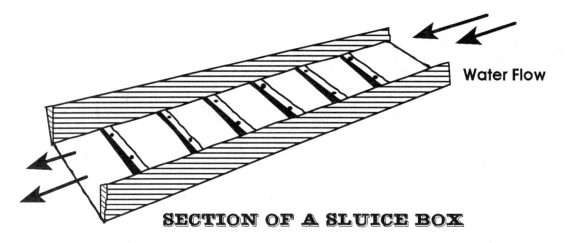

Water Flow

SECTION OF A SLUICE BOX

When placer gold was not as easy to find, miners searched for the source of the yellow mineral that was locked inside quartz. From the earliest days of **hardrock mining** a strong back and steady nerves were needed by miners who brought up **ore** from underground tunnels they dug deep into the earth. This type of mining required expensive equipment and was dangerous because of the use of explosives and constant threat of cave-ins or fires. Even so, thousands of dark mine shafts were chiseled throughout the Mother Lode during the course of the Gold Rush. But after the profitable yellow-streaked rock was brought up to the light of day, only half of the victory was won.

As the broken chunks of ore were carted to the surface, it still had to be crushed to extract the gold. Miners who could not afford costly equipment to harness water or buy steam engines to power their mills found other creative ways to grind their quartz. For example, some clever individuals simply tied a rope to the branch of a young tree that could be bent over. Then the free end of the rope was tied to a heavy, solid, iron cylinder that was positioned over pieces of ore sitting on a metal plate. By pulling hard on the rope, the iron crusher would smash the rocks as the strong, flexible tree branch made the weight easy to pull up again. The bits of crushed rock would then have to be separated by hand to get the small flakes of gold it released. Needless to say this method was not very efficient because it was so time consuming, and the ore would have to be especially rich since tons would have to be crushed in order to turn a profit. Fortunately, there were other more practical and inexpensive methods available to hardrock miners – knowledge brought to California by experienced gold seekers from other countries.

ARRASTRA

It was the Mexicans who developed a crusher that could effectively grind a profitable quantity of ore and was available to anyone who owned a work animal. The arrastra was a simple mill that consisted of a level, circular stone floor surrounded by a low wall. A strong wooden post was then mounted in the center. After another sturdy pole was fastened horizontally to the center post like a propeller, a heavy slice of flat rock was bolted to a chain and attached to the middle of it. An animal, hitched to the outside end of the pole, dependably walked around and around the outside of the wall powering the stone slab as it crunched over finger-sized pieces of ore. At the close of a long day for both men and animals, the grain-size quartz mixed with tiny flecks of gold would be scraped up from within the basin into buckets and taken to a stream. There the small particles of yellow would be washed out from the waste rock, and the miner would bag his profits.

California State Library Archive

CHILEAN WHEEL

The Chileans of South America brought over their own clever idea of grinding ore, too. Called the Chilean wheel, it worked exactly like the arrastra. However, instead of the animals dragging a flat slab of rock, the skilled workers from this Latin country neatly carved a circular stone wheel anywhere from five to ten feet in diameter. On a twenty-four inch wide crushing surface, the miners attached an iron ring, placed a metal axle through a cut in center of the disk, then harnessed the animals to a wooden hitch who pulled the wheel around a circular iron floor basin. The advantages of the "Chile mill" made it possible to crush more than five tons of ore in a day, and the smoothness of the two metal surfaces allowed the heavy wheel to efficiently release most of the prime gold held in the rock. The one drawback to the Chilean Wheel was that it was difficult to profit from low grade ore. And it wouldn't be too long before more advanced machines completely dominated hardrock mining.

To make the process of separating the gold from crushed ore easier, liquid **mercury**, also called quicksilver, was commonly being utilized throughout the Mother Lode since it sticks to gold but not rock. As a result, it became very popular with miners who applied it to remove the profits from their valuable grit. This saved them countless hours they would have normally spent using only water to complete the same job.

California State Library Archive

47

STAMP MILL

The stamp mill originated in Germany where it was used to crush coal, but the miners in California put the same idea to work for extracting gold. The earliest 49ers harnessed water to power their first crude stamps, but by the middle 1850's the smoke from wood that fed steam boilers filled the air as hundreds of noisy mills with their mechanical rattles could be heard throughout the Mother Lode.

One-thousand pound metal rods or stamps with replaceable iron "shoes" hammered ore 24 hours a day without objection. The largest operations could crush up to 700 tons during that period! Working in sets of two or as many as 80, these "batteries" were fed baseball sized chunks of quartz hoisted to the top of the mill by a cable drawn cart. When dumped, gravity and the endless clatter of moving parts powered by the steam engine caused the ore to fall to the bottom of a funnel-shaped hopper. Here it shook through a metal grating called a "grizzly" whose purpose was to filter out occasional large pieces of ore that would cause a jam in the crushing area. A horizontal drive shaft attached to a belt driven wheel turned cams near the top of the stamp posts which lifted and dropped them into a water filled trough. There the sized rock was pulverized into a runny, buttermilk-colored mix known as "slurry." An operator, deafened by the methodical sound of the stamps, watched to make sure the process ran smoothly.

The ceaseless pounding of the machine sloshed the now liquefied contents through an ultra fine screen mesh insuring that the ore was thoroughly smashed before it ran over a gently angled tray made of copper. If you remember, mercury clings to gold; it also sticks to copper. So before milling began, a miner would brush on a thin film of the liquid metal onto the tray. This arrangement allowed the waste rock to pass over the mercury coating while it captured thousands of nearly invisible specks of gold.

The operator had to know when to stop the mill and collect his profits. For if the layer of quicksilver became too loaded with gold, it would begin to break apart and slip down the tray into the **tailings** pile and be all but lost. An experienced miner knew just when to stop crushing the ore and scrape off the heavy clay-like mixture called **amalgam** before preparing the copper surface once again. The questionable looking dull grey ball containing gold would then be stored away until the bonded metals were ready to be separated with heat.

Front view of stamp mill located in Mariposa

RETORT

After the amalgam had been collected, the next step was to separate the softball-sized metallic glob by heating it in a boiler known as a retort. The process began when the amalgam was placed in a sealed chamber and heated to molten temperatures. Since gold liquefies at a much higher degree, the mercury vaporized first leaving the gold behind. The evaporated quicksilver then moved through a long iron tube attached to a closed chamber where it cooled and returned to its original form. A water filled bucket at the end of the pipe captured the gathering droplets so it could be used again.

When the heating chamber was safe to open, an air-bubbled plug of gold resembling a sponge remained for all the miners' time consuming work. Retorts came in a variety of different designs, but all of them were very dangerous to use. Inhaled mercury fumes can cause numerous health problems ranging from liver to nerve damage, and in large amounts it can even cause death. Years of simply handling the substance could end in poisonous complications because it was absorbed through the skin. Quicksilver was widely used in the years of the Gold Rush, and it was no mistake that great care was observed during the division of these two fascinating metals of attraction.

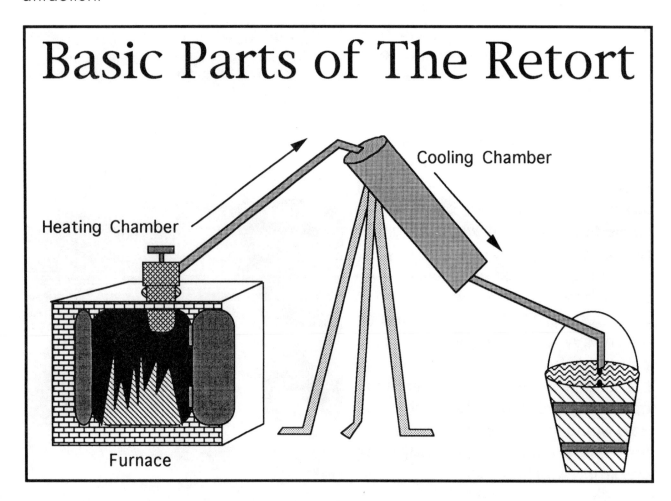

Basic Parts of The Retort

Cooling Chamber

Heating Chamber

Furnace

HYDRAULIC MINING

Hydraulic mining was born in California. It began in 1852 when a French-Canadian named Antoine Chabot (who didn't like shoveling) devised a hand-sewn canvas hose to wash loose, muddy gravels into his sluice box. A year later an American, Edward Mattison, refined the developing technique by adding a metal nozzle to the end of a similar hose. His improvement created a punch of water that was able to blast away at much harder gold bearing sediments locked inside hillsides.

By the late 1860's crude stovepipe and canvas hoses were being replaced with riveted sections of heavy iron pipes. Starting out at a diameter of thirty inches and decreasing to twelve or less over its length, this system harnessed the water's incredible power. A cannon-like nozzle called

California State Library Archive

a "monitor" or "giant" with an outlet of up to eight inches was attached to the end of a swivel neck that completed this relatively Spartan device. The opening of a valve allowed the force of gravity to propel an available supply of liquid energy through the penstock (pipeline) that snaked down the side of a hill. The concentration of water that violently erupted from the monitor smashed away at hardened gravel deposits creating a muddy sludge called "slickens" which was washed or hauled into long sluice boxes. About once a month or so the millions of tiny gold particles trapped behind hundreds of riffle bars would be collected and melted into ingots (bars) that were sold at the current price.

To aim the monitor, operators simply pointed the nozzle in the direction they wanted it to go. Using as little effort as it would take to close a car door, the monitor was easy to guide but could be very deadly if a man or animal crossed its lethal path even as far away as two-hundred feet. So powerful was the water that exploded from these giants, that a man striking the dynamic jet with a crowbar could not penetrate it. The force of energy was so great that boulders weighing more than fifty pounds were tossed about like enormous ping-pong balls. It is little wonder that sediments as hard as concrete could be blasted away efficiently and with great speed.

50

In addition to natural lakes and streams, thousands of miles of ditches, dams and reservoirs were built to tap the vast quantities of water needed for hydraulic mining operations. This led to the creation of dozens of water companies who controlled the reserves of potential power sold to mines, lumber and saw mills. Eventually some of these companies extended their services to the agricultural lands of the San Joaquin Valley and made large-scale irrigation possible. With the development of electric generators, the miles of canals and reservoirs were quickly converted to fit the needs for an inexpensive source of power. They provided convenient, ready-made energy for the people of foothill towns, even before more progressive cities like San Francisco.

Hydraulic mining was very economical. If an outfit earned only a few cents worth of gold from a piece of ground as big as a bathtub, it was profitable. Unfortunately, this type of mining had disastrous effects on the environment. Massive areas of land were scarred into lifeless pits and rendered useless for any other purpose. The muddy sludge that passed over the sluice boxes had to be dumped somewhere, and it was usually led to a river. Cloudy sediments replaced the once clean, free-flowing water of all major streams in the Northern Mother Lode as silty masses of thick brown of debris filled their channels.

The long term consequences of hydraulic wastes were unmistakable. Riverboat travel was impaired on notable rivers like the Yuba and American, fish were suffocated and animal habitats devastated. When spring snow melt added more water to the already choked riverbeds, many overflowed and flooded choice farmlands or destroyed communities. Some highland canyons actually clogged with the heavy muck. If they spilled over untold lives certainly would have been lost in settlements below during the tremendous mudslide that would have followed. The voice of public outrage slowly gathered strength.

A long legal battle over the effects that hydraulic mining had on the environment and communities ended in 1884 when Judge Alonzo Sawyer ruled that the use of these powerful hoses would have to stop unless waste materials could be contained. This decision resulted in the closure of all but a handful of hydraulic operations in the coming years. Today, the many scars that these water cannons left behind remain as permanent signatures on the countryside forever marking this turbulent time.

California State Library Archive

DREDGING

Countless bits and pieces of placer gold remained deep within the unreachable sediments of Mother Lode riverbeds. The problem, however, was to develop a reliable method of scooping up or dredging huge quantities of these gravels and make a profit. As early as 1849, a crude, steam powered dredge was transported around the tip of South America to California; but almost as soon as it was assembled and operating, it sank to the bottom of the Sacramento River. Another version appeared in 1850 when a small river steamer named the Phoenix was outfitted with a chain of buckets and put to use on the Yuba River near Marysville; its failure was that it proved too costly and was quickly abandoned. Other attempts followed but with similar disappointing results.

California State Library Archive

The earliest dredges that had any success were used in New Zealand in the 1860's, but it would be many years of trial and error before the Golden State would see its first profitable dredge. Eventually borrowed ideas, advancements in technology and large sums of invested money helped create California's first dependable, highly mechanized dredge in 1898. This steam powered vessel scraped out the rich placer deposits of the Feather River near Oroville with excellent results. In the coming years, these massive, boxy machines became more and more common as the mechanical chains that linked a series of buckets retrieved millions of dollars in gold from river gravels throughout the state.

By 1901 electricity had replaced steam power as large-scale operations continued. Waterproof cables that were able to flex with the motions of the dredge provided the necessary energy more dependably and conveniently as the industry expanded.

These noisy machines were by far the most complicated of all types of placer mining. They worked essentially like giant mechanical sluice boxes sifting through tons of hidden gravel deposits for the tiny bits of yellow metal that all added up to huge profits. And although dredges came in a variety of sizes and all worked basically the same, it was the largest ones that attracted the most attention. A typical big dredge was 100 feet long from end to end, 40 feet wide and stood some 50 feet above the water level. It was built mainly of iron with an external frame covered by tin or wood panels similar to a houseboat. It weighed more than 3000 tons! Some of these raft-like giants had one-hundred scoop buckets linked in line by a rotating chain. This in turn was supported by an iron hoist called a gantry which made it possible to adjust the digging angle down to a depth of 75 feet. Each bucket was about the size of small hot tub and weighed in at 2000 pounds. If a bucket yielded a 30 cent profit on the average, it was considered productive in the early 1900's. Amazingly these monoliths required only three men on board to operate. On the other hand, a land support crew of twenty or more were constantly welding and repairing broken parts or keeping up with needed maintenance.

When the buckets delivered their muddy contents to the main body, the interior was designed to efficiently separate the gravel and gold like a huge washing machine. Unearthed sediments were channeled into a large, open-ended cylinder made of heavy-duty iron pierced with thousands of quarter inch holes. Mounted horizontally at a slight angle, it slowly rotated on gears. High pressure water jets blasted the disorderly mixture from a metal pipe suspended through the middle of the cylinder. After being rinsed, the waste rocks that tumbled to the end of the drum were carried off on a long conveyor belt called a stacker. This arm extended behind the dredge and deposited the rocks in great mounds called tailings piles.

Mud, rock, sand and gold that filtered through the cylinder's holes passed over an enormous system of metal sluice boxes as thousands of gallons of water flushed over the moving jumble of sludge. Hundreds of riffle bars trapped the heavier gold while lighter materials flowed out an opening in the side of the dredge into a watery pit where it sat. About once a week, millions of tiny gold particles would be shoveled out from behind the many riffles and melted into bars on the spot in preparation to be sold.

These immense iron rafts had to be stabilized when in use, and it was done in simple but ingenious ways. A large cable-controlled spike called a "spud", located toward the back center of the dredge, could be vertically raised or lowered into the pit. The weight of this 30 foot long iron spike secured the main body and kept the entire machine from lurching forward while digging but allowed it to pivot. Also, if needed, reels of thickly wound metal cables mounted on the front of the dredge could be anchored to land keeping drift to a minimum. With everything in place, the bucket-line rotated as the machine slowly dug from side to side, gouging a self-made pit. When the spud was raised the bucket-line arm could then drag the main body into new territory for excavation.

Dredges were not limited to riverbeds; they could operate anywhere the water table was close to the surface. But after an area was worked out, all of the topsoil was displaced and only mounds of bare rock tailings covered the landscape rendering it useless for any other purpose. Dredging continued throughout the 1900's reaching its peak during the 1930's. But in the following decade the government suspended all gold mining operations during World War II because they were not an essential industry to the war effort. After the war, dredging once again resumed, but the enormous maintenance costs and relatively low price of gold at the time were collapsing the industry.

In addition to the setback caused by the war, new concerns about the environment were also emerging. Some new regional laws stated that companies had to level out tailings and replace the topsoil of areas they worked. This delivered a final blow for many enterprises.

On October 1, 1968 the last dredge took its final grinding bite near Oroville marking the end of an era in California. But the unmistakable monuments left behind throughout the state are still here to remind us of the variety of mining techniques used to pursue men's dreams of wealth. They highlight a period of our nation's development that uniquely stands out from all other landscapes in history.

Massive piles of tailings line a road at the edge of the gold country

54

SELF-TEST: MINING TECHNIQUES

A. Name the six techniques miners used to recover *placer* gold:

1. _____   4. _____
2. _____   5. _____
3. _____   6. _____

B. Name three *hardrock* mining devices that crushed quartz ore:

1. _____   2. _____   3. _____

C. Describe how a retort separates amalgam: _____
_____
_____
_____
_____
_____
_____

D. Write the name of the mining instrument that fits these words below:

1. GANTRY _____   5. APRON _____
2. MONITOR _____   6. SPUD _____
3. FLUME _____   7. SLURRY _____
4. RIDDLE _____   8. SLICKENS _____

E. Name one of the techniques you read about explaining how cooperation between miners could improve their rewards: _____
_____
_____
_____
_____

F. Which technology was the most destructive to the environment? Why?
_____
_____
_____
_____
_____

*The photograph on page 41 shows four different methods described in <u>Mining Techniques</u>. Use it as you explain to an interested listener how these techniques worked. Be sure to include in your discussion the advantages, disadvantages or environmental consequences of each one.

55

MINING METHODS CROSSWORD
PUZZLE

SIDEWAYS OR BACKWARDS

1. Each crusher weighed 1000 lbs.

5. Another name for mercury.

6. Used a series of riffle bars to trap gold.

7. This machine left behind large piles of rock called "tailings."

8. The most basic way miners collected gold.

10. This method forced water through a "monitor."

UP OR DOWN

2. A mule pulled a stone to crush the gold ore.

3. Gravels were channeled down a trough before they ran over the riddle.

4. Type of rock crushed by a Chilean wheel.

9. Also called a cradle.

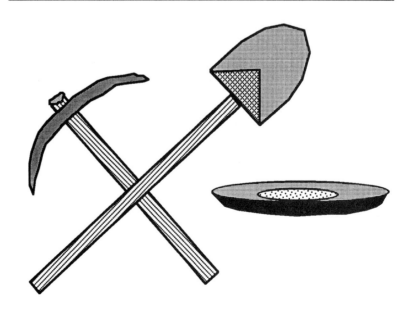

56

THE PONY EXPRESS AND TELEGRAPH

"Here he comes! Away across the endless dead level of the prairie a black speck appears against the sky . . . . sweeping toward us nearer and nearer . . . . a whoop and a hurrah . . . . a wave of the rider's hand . . . . a man and a horse burst past our excited faces, and go winging away like the [last] fragment of a storm!" Thus were the words of Mark Twain upon seeing a Pony Express rider from his stagecoach heading west in 1861. It might have seemed as though this rugged type of life was glamorous, but that was rarely the case. Many of the riders were between 15 to 20 years of age and rode an average of 65 jolting miles a day changing horses about every 10 miles at relay stations as they brought news to and from California.

The idea of the Pony Express began with a Missouri businessman by the name of William Russell. He knew that people in the west craved news and letters from loved ones in the east almost as much as gold. The problem was that thousands of miles separated California from the rest of the nation and the fastest stagecoach took three weeks at best to reach the state while steamships took twice that long. Russell's solution was simple; he believed that by setting up relay stations along a route nearly 2000 miles long, he could bring the mail from St. Joseph, Missouri to Sacramento, California in as little as ten days which was unheard of at the time.

To achieve his goal, Russell and his business partners hired some 80 riders and bought about 400 horses. They would be placed at 157 relay stations along a route the emigrants had been struggling through for years. In addition, stock tenders, station keepers, trail supervisors and supply wagons were organized to support this ambitious task. The expert riders chosen for the job were young and lightweight, many under 130 pounds, and had to be willing to risk their lives for the sum of about $60 dollars a month plus bonuses. There was no shortage of riders and on April 3, 1860 the Pony Express began its first westbound run from St. Joseph with the sounds of a cheering crowd and a cannon blast.

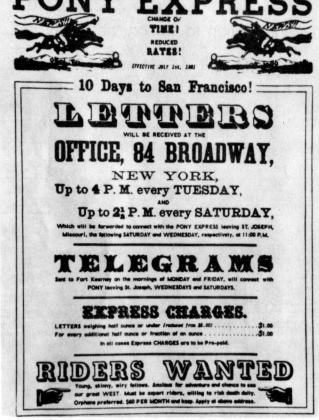

Russell's plan was a success. The first mail reached Sacramento in just under ten days, and San Francisco letters were carried by steamboat from Sutter's Fort the following afternoon. The Express proved its worth, and the faithful riders regularly dashed east and west once a week and soon eight times a month. Californians were now all but guaranteed a closeness with the rest of the country.

This closeness did not come cheap, however. Mail was first carried at $10.00 an ounce. An average letter weighed about half that, but in order to compete for more business the price was later lowered to $2.00 an ounce. Riders carried their payload in a specially designed saddle cover called a "mochila" which means knapsack in Spanish. It was a rectangular shaped leather apron with pouches sewn on all four corners. The bags could be filled with a little more than twenty pounds of various letters, telegrams, and newspapers printed on tissue thin paper. Only the rider's weight held it on, and it could be whisked off in seconds for a change of horses.

As a rider traveled farther west connecting station to station, his safety became more uncertain. The native Paiutes living in what is now Nevada and western Utah became alarmed at the numbers of new people crossing over or taking their land. Relations between the natives and

Mochila

Illustration of mochila over a saddle

Actual weight of saddle and empty mochila, 13 pounds

the settlers became hostile, and Express riders were exposed to the dangers of attack. Equipped only with the protection of a knife and a six-shooter to keep weight at a minimum, the young riders crossed Paiute territory with nervous caution. Eventual conflicts resulted in one rider's death, several relay stations burned, and some 19 other employees killed by natives.

If Indian attack wasn't an immediate concern, the weather was another hazard that challenged the courage of the young men. More than once, knee deep snow or swollen rivers slowed, but rarely stopped, the determination of riders crossing mountain passes and plains. In its 19 months of service, only one mochila was ever lost in over 150 demanding trips.

Two of the better known riders who whisked mochilas from saddles to horses were James Butler Hickock and William F. Cody. Each achieved early fame during his employment with the Express. "Wild Bill" Hickock, as he became known, claimed to have fought a bear in hand-to-hand combat and was also involved in a gunfight that ended in the deaths of several men. Billy Cody, on the other hand, earned his reputation at the age of 15 and best describes one of his rides through the Rocky Mountains in his own words:

"One day when I galloped into Three Crossings, my home station, I found that the rider who was expected to take the trip out...had been killed; and that there was no one to take his place. I did not hesitate for a moment to undertake an extra ride of eighty-five miles [through South Pass] to Rocky Ridge, and I arrived...on time. Then, I turned back and rode to Red Buttes, my starting place...a distance of 322 miles."

Cody later became the famous "Buffalo Bill" known for his wild west show that entertained thousands while the real west became an image of the past as towns grew and the law was enforced. "Wild Bill" Hickock became a sheriff in Deadwood, South Dakota where he did his best to carry out law and order. But as the two men aged they surely could never forget the excitement, hardship and peril that every rider experienced during his career with the Express.

Life-size statue of a Pony Express rider in Old Sacramento

Yet what the best man and horse could do in 1861 quickly fell behind a faster method of sending news to the west. The telegraph had been used in the eastern states and California long before 1860, but now a new wire was being strung along the Express route's path. Crews working east and west were hurriedly connecting a transcontinental line which was to meet at Salt Lake City, Utah. By October 1861 the job was finished. Soon messages and news were dot-dashed over geography in minutes reducing the need for land transportation. After delivering nearly 35,000 pieces of mail, huge expenses and failure to ever make a profit had ruined the Pony Express.

Within a week after the completion of the Atlantic-Pacific telegraph line, the last mochila was relayed across familiar territory ending the short but famous history of the Pony Express. The San Francisco Pacific newspaper summed up many people's feelings in a final tribute in 1861 . . . **"We have looked for you as those who wait for the morning, and how seldom did you fail us! When days were months and hours weeks, how you thrilled us out of our pain and suspense, to know the best or the worst! You have served us well!"**

SELF-TEST: PONY EXPRESS

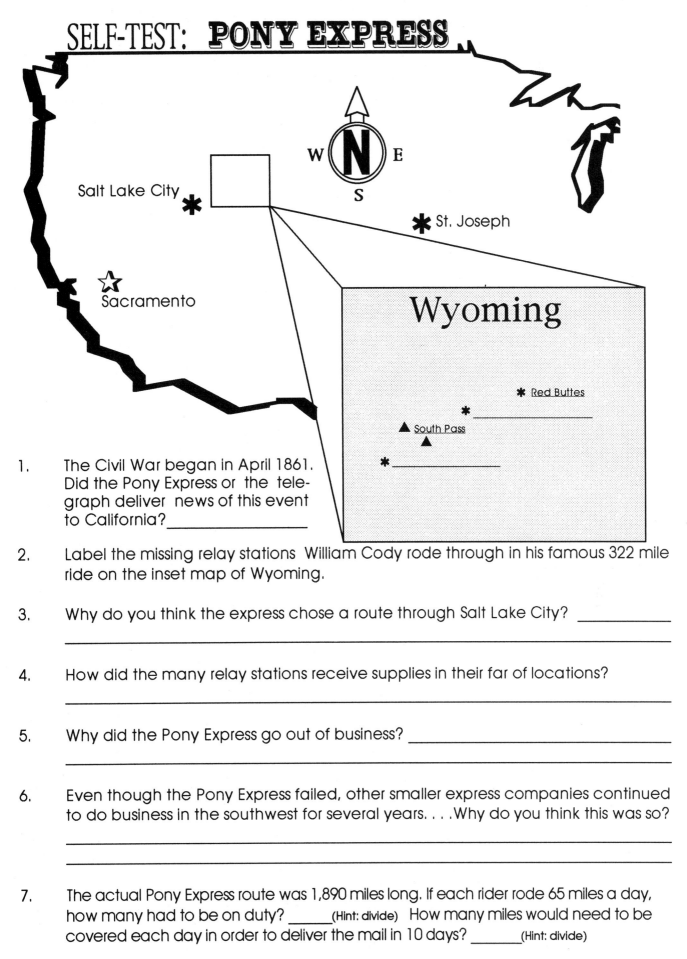

Salt Lake City ✳

☆
Sacramento

✳ St. Joseph

Wyoming

✳ Red Buttes

✳ _____

▲ South Pass
▲

✳ _____

1. The Civil War began in April 1861. Did the Pony Express or the telegraph deliver news of this event to California?_____

2. Label the missing relay stations William Cody rode through in his famous 322 mile ride on the inset map of Wyoming.

3. Why do you think the express chose a route through Salt Lake City? _____
_____

4. How did the many relay stations receive supplies in their far of locations?
_____

5. Why did the Pony Express go out of business? _____
_____

6. Even though the Pony Express failed, other smaller express companies continued to do business in the southwest for several years. . . .Why do you think this was so?
_____
_____

7. The actual Pony Express route was 1,890 miles long. If each rider rode 65 miles a day, how many had to be on duty? _____(Hint: divide) How many miles would need to be covered each day in order to deliver the mail in 10 days? _____(Hint: divide)

It wasn't until 1843 that the telegraph began connecting cities in the eastern states. By the early 1850's the growing towns of California began sending messages with the electronic dots and dashes of a code developed mainly by Samuel B. Morse as well. But the large expanse of land between Fort Kearney, Nebraska all the way to Carson City, Nevada was not yet united by the technology. The services of steamboats, stagecoaches and newly formed Pony Express were required to carry all communications west. Although they filled the gap, delivery by any of those methods could not speed information quickly enough for news hungry Californians. The only solution was to build a transcontinental telegraph that would once and for all link the vast western space separating the nation.

Construction of the evenly spaced poles, wooden insulators and bare wires that would span the length from central Nebraska to western Nevada began in 1860. Two groups of government funded workers raced each other from opposite ends of the country setting up the thin line that would bring the states closer together and finish off the bankrupt the Pony Express nearly as fast. In only five months, the crews made final connections on October 24, 1861 in Salt Lake City nine months ahead of schedule. Shortly thereafter in San Francisco, Stephen J. Field, a California judge, who took the place of the absent governor, read California's first official transcontinental message. In the midst of a crowded room a technician clicked his words on a sender that relayed them over a wire to New York in record time. Suddenly a battery powered technology had made coast to coast communications a simple task that took only minutes instead of a luxury that was counted in days. Remarkably, a crude telegraph line had swiftly changed the face of our nation.

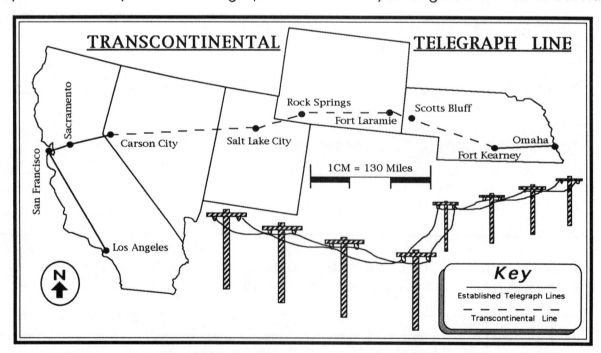

TRANSCONTINENTAL   TELEGRAPH   LINE

Rock Springs
Fort Laramie
Scotts Bluff
Carson City
Salt Lake City
Omaha
Fort Kearney
Sacramento
San Francisco
Los Angeles

1CM = 130 Miles

N

Key
Established Telegraph Lines
- - - - - Transcontinental Line

*To find out what Judge Field's first message was about, use the Morse Code Key to decipher his words on the following page:

MORSE CODE KEY

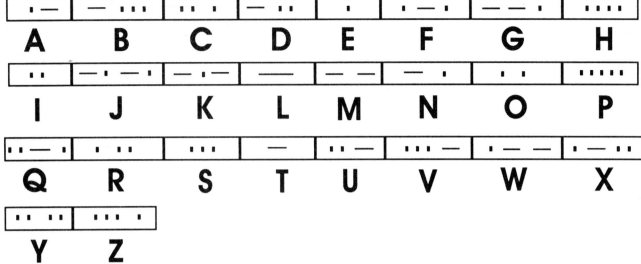

******** (Decode Judge Field's Message The On Lines Below) ********

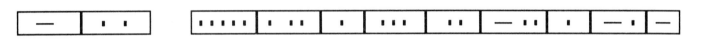

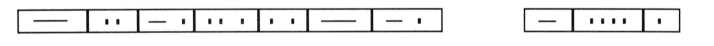

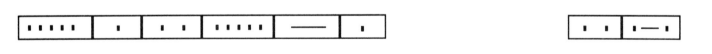

AMERICAN INVENTORS OF THE 1800's

	DATE	INVENTION	INVENTOR
1)	**1807**	**1st Practical Steamboat**	**Robert Fulton**
2)	1830	T-Rail Train Track	Robert Stevens
3)	**1834**	**1st Mechanical Refrigerator**	**Jacob Perkins**
4)	1840	Photography Studio	Alexander Wolcott
5)	**1843**	**Produced Flexible Rubber**	**Charles Goodyear**
6)	1849	Safety Pin	Walter Hunt
7)	**1854**	**Can Opener**	**Ezra Warner**
8)	1867	Potato Chips	Hyram S.Thomas
9)	**1876**	**Telephone**	**Alexander Graham Bell**
10)	1879	Light Bulb	Thomas A. Edison
11)	**1886**	**Coca-Cola**	**Dr. Joseph Pemberton**
12)	1893	Zipper	Whitcomb Judson

ACTIVITY: Cut out 12 squares of paper about 2x2 inches each writing the invention on one side and inventor on the other to make flashcards that will help you remember the things that helped make our world better.

INTRODUCTION TO TOWNS OF THE MOTHER LODE

The following pages contain a location map and brief history of over 30 selected Gold Rush towns. Most are found along modern highway 49, which is the same trail thousands of prospectors took as they wandered from camp to camp throughout the Mother Lode in search of gold. A majority of these tent towns developed into thriving communities where modern structures now stand among the traces of slate stone foundations or crumbling adobe walls. Still, many other once lively villages faded into seldom remembered ghost towns.

Even today the countryside between the settlements of this foothill region testifies to the heyday of the Gold Rush. Numerous abandoned mines shafts, remains of rusted equipment and piles of rocky debris quietly lay scattered throughout the area. There are also more mysterious reminders, too. Long stretches of mortarless stone fences carefully built by the Chinese aimlessly span miles of uncrowded hills over rugged territory. Their nearly forgotten purpose was to mark property lines or corral livestock. Now, as in the past, a wealth of interesting sights awaits anyone with a watchful eye and desire to explore.

If possible try to visit these and other Mother Lode towns in order to examine, discover, and get a first-hand personal sense of history from this era. Use the map key on the next page to locate each place as you read the upcoming selection.

MOTHER LODE TOWNS AND LOCATIONS

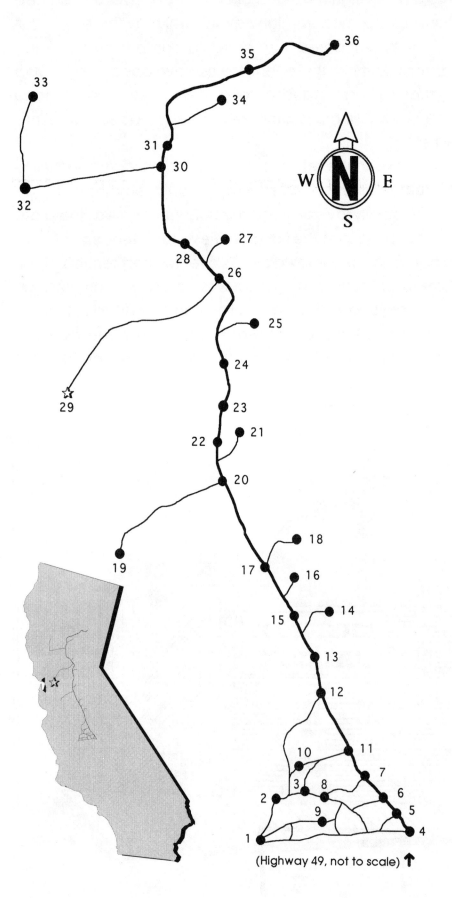

(Highway 49, not to scale)

MERCED

This is where our tour begins. The San Joaquin Valley where many Californians call home is shaped from a basin of natural beauty. John Muir, the famous naturalist who helped preserve Yosemite, crossed near this area in the spring of 1868. He described the region as, "One smooth, continuous bed of honeybloom, so marvelously rich that in walking from one end of it to the other... your foot would press about a hundred flowers at every step." Native Americans also once populated these level, semi-arid grasslands and wetlands where migratory birds once darkened the sky. Long since altered, this central plain supported the farms, and its pastures nourished cattle and sheep the new settlers would bring.

By 1872 an extension of the Central Pacific Railroad passed through the settlement of Merced paving the way for its growth. Railroad officials determined that this would be a good jumping off point for tourists going to Yosemite Valley, so they sold the surrounding land to investors at high prices. That same year, a hotel named the Cosmopolitan was constructed to meet the needs of visitors; it had 175 rooms! Unfortunately, it burned down in 1929.

In 1874 a courthouse was built thus establishing Merced's place on the map. No gold was ever found at this location, but agriculture has been even more profitable. And just like other towns throughout the valley, dirt roads leading to the foothills of the Mother Lode helped supply the needs of miners until that era came to an end.

SNELLING

It's hard to believe that the little town of Snelling was once home to thousands of people with Merced county's first courthouse, several stores, a hotel, blacksmiths, 4 lawyers, 2 doctors and a teacher. Today the town's population is only a fraction of what it was, but Snelling happened to be at a good location on a route that supplied miners in the Southern Mother Lode. It prospered for that reason during the 1850's.

Just east of Snelling was another important small community named Merced Falls. It was here that sheep and cattle could cross the Merced River and a trading post flourished. Soon, due to the region's plentiful wheat crop, a flour mill was built using the Merced River for power. The town thrived as a woolen mill and an iron **foundry** were promptly constructed. Unfortunately, the area was prone to disasters such as flooding, and in 1895 a fire nearly destroyed the entire community.

The town survived when a saw mill began operations in the early 1900's once again reviving local businesses. The Yosemite Valley Railroad supplied the mill with logs brought down from the Sierra as blades rotated 24 hours a day. Dredging in the region also took place; however, by the 1940's a shortage of trees, the failing railroad, and dredging restrictions soon doomed the ill-fated town, Snelling was also affected. Today only the shells of Merced Falls' lumber buildings exist beside piles of dredge tailings, but Snelling remains as a small farming and service community.

MARIPOSA

It was John C. Fremont, the famed explorer, army officer and politician, who purchased a huge region of 40,000 acres from the Mexican government before war broke out between the two countries. After gold was rediscovered in 1848, he "floated" the unrestricted property lines of his $3000 investment to include the rich mines surrounding Mariposa. This area made Fremont a millionaire, but in the end he lost it all. A true Mother Lode town, Mariposa rapidly grew from a small settlement originally named Logtown into a county seat that covered 30,000 miles. By 1854 Mariposa had its own courthouse, the oldest in the state, where many current mining laws were established, and a weekly newspaper. Both are still in operation today. Visit Mariposa's excellent museum for a true flash of the past. (See Appendix B, Page 101)

Mariposa, the largest of California's original 27 counties

MOUNT BULLION

This was not a very large town, but $3 million in gold was taken from its famous Princeton Mine. The type of mining that took place was called hardrock or quartz mining, and it was said that a person riding a horse in the late 1850's could hear the noisy rattle of stamp mills non-stop from here to Lake Tahoe!

MOUNT OPHIR

It is a popular myth that eight-sided $50 gold coins were privately minted here by the assayer John L. Moffat and Co., but those coins were never struck at this location. The legend was simply an attempt to create tourism in the area that was promoted in part by a local newspaper. It did, however, encourage would-be treasure hunters who destroyed the remaining buildings in their ruthless search for non-existent gold. Mount Ophir was in truth a hardrock mine that was moderately productive. Like many other tent towns that grew almost overnight and disappeared nearly as quickly when the gold was gone, Mount Ophir was able to quietly survive as a small supply center before becoming a complete ghost town. Only the ruins of a few slate stone walls and foundations entombed in thick underbrush remain.

BEAR VALLEY

In the early 1850's Bear Valley had a population of about 3000. This was where its most famous citizen John C. Fremont built a home many called the "White House" since he attempted the presidency in 1856. He also had a hotel built where luxury was in style. In 1863, Fremont sold his land grant for $6 million to pay debts. His house fell into disrepair and the hotel burned to the ground. Where famous people, wealth, and miner's shacks once stood, only a small population remains today.

The slate stone remains of the Bear Valley jail. When in use, a large iron eyelet embedded in the cell's concrete floor provided a secure hold for threading the chain of the prisoner's ankle cuffs making escape less likely.

SELF-TEST: MERCED TO BEAR VALLEY

1. Describe the San Joaquin Valley before it was altered: _____
    _____
    _____
    _____
    _____

2. What was Snelling like before its decline? _____
    _____
    _____
    _____

3. Name three types of mills that operated in Merced Falls: _____
    _____

    a. What kind of disaster destroyed the town in 1895? _____

    b. Why did Merced Falls lose its importance? _____
        _____
        _____

4. Name two organizations that have operated in Mariposa since the Gold Rush:
    _____

    a. What was Mariposa's other name? _____

5. Name the type of mining that took place at Mount Bullion: _____

6. What town never produced $50 gold coins? _____

    a. Why was the rumor started? _____
    _____

    b. What happened as a result of this rumor? _____
    _____

7. Describe how large Mariposa County was at one time: _____
    _____
    _____

8. Who lived in the residence known as the "White House?" _____

    a. Briefly tell about his life in the Mother Lode: _____
        _____
        _____
        _____
        _____
        _____
        _____

HORNITOS

This town's name means "Little Ovens," which probably refers to the oven-shaped burial chambers that the Mexicans constructed above ground. Nevertheless, it became one of the most heck-raising places of the Mother Lode. With a population of 5,000 by the early 1850's, this town supported four hotels, thirty-six saloons and six stores. It included Domingo Ghirardelli's store who later became famous making chocolate candy in San Francisco. At one time thousands of dollars every month in rough gold was being shipped from here by Wells Fargo stagecoaches. Its collection office is in ruins today. Hornitos was also known for its lawlessness and vices. The town's Spanish-style plaza was once the scene of gambling tables, dances, and killings. It also claimed to be a haven for bandits real and imagined. Hornitos is nearly abandoned today, but it remains one of the few towns that gives visitors a true sense of history.

Remains of adobe wall in background reflects Spanish influence in Hornitos

INDIAN GULCH

This tent town was originally named Santa Cruz by the Mexican miners who first settled here. Today, only three buildings remain, but once there were two hotels, several stores, a blacksmith's shop, saloons and gambling halls. It was never a very productive area and many buildings fell into disrepair. Santa Cruz became known as Indian Gulch with only a few saloons and store remaining. With time, this "town" became a refuge for horse and cattle thieves. The penalty for stealing those animals was usually death because it took away a person's ability to make a living. Getting caught quickly shortened a thief's life at the end of a rope. Sometimes a murderer would be released if he had a good reason for killing another person, but rarely would there be a pardon for "horse thieving." The town was kept alive into the 1930's until its last store owner, Nicola Solari, passed away. Today a rancher's sheep graze in the solitude of this once thriving town.

LA GRANGE

This place was originally settled by French miners around 1850. When the easy gold was taken, a new way of mining was introduced – hydraulic. If you get a chance to visit La Grange, look at the surrounding landscape. You will notice the sides of hills in the area seem to be eroding naturally. To a point this is correct; however, these hills had some help because water cannons were used extensively to blast away at the ancient riverbed sediments of the Tuolumne River, so miners could get at the precious gold they sought.

La Grange also had at least one famous person you might have heard about by the name of Bret Harte. He was just eighteen years old when he taught school here for a short time in 1854 but later became famous writing about the Gold Rush and the people who lived it. One of his better known stories is titled The Outcasts of Poker Flat.

In 1917 large-scale dredging was established in the area. Just outside town you can still see the rusted hull of one called the "Grey Goose". It has been dismantled and little of it remains today, but when in use, this 3000 ton monolith stood nearly fifty feet high and washed out countless tons of gold-bearing gravels. This machine went out of service in the early 1940's, but the piles of tailings it left behind remain as enduring signs of the past.

COULTERVILLE

At the time gold was discovered this Mexican dominated village quickly burst into a tent town that wandering prospectors and merchants found especially prosperous. Miners of several nationalities rapidly populated the area including many Chinese who were lured by rich placer streams. George W. Coulter set up a supply store at this location in 1850, and his blue canvas tent became a well-known landmark. Even though the settlement had other names in its past, it eventually adopted Coulter's because of his notable recognition. Fires burned main street to the ground three times over the years, but the town always rebounded because hardrock mining continued to bring the region prosperity well into the 1900's. Getting ore from the hillside mines to the mills was always an ever present challenge, but the difficulty was solved in part by machine technology when the Merced Mining Company purchased a small steam engine in 1897. Built in Pittsburgh, Pennsylvania it was transported around the horn of South America to San Francisco where it was carried in sections by mule train to Coulterville. There it was put to work hauling ore from steep mountainside mines puffing along on narrow iron tracks. That same engine,

the "Whistling Billy," is currently on display outside the historical museum next to Highway 49.

In its long past this town served as a stopover for travelers on their way to Yosemite Valley until more direct roads guided them away. Today Coulterville is important because it is considered an historical landmark where several original buildings remain like the Chinese Sun Sun Wo store built of adobe brick in 1851. Modernization has been slow to change this community since the late 1800's.

CHINESE CAMP

The Chinese were probably the most persecuted ethnic group in the Mother Lode. Their culture, language and dress was so different from the overwhelming numbers of European Americans, they could be easily singled out. The groups of Chinese mining companies who settled this area generally escaped abuse, and they also found rich gold deposits. Six years later in 1856 Chinese Camp became the hub of several transportation routes and had a population of about 5000. However, this was also when the town's two major "tongs" (secret Chinese societies) began quarreling among themselves. The argument was probably over mining rights, but whatever the reason about

Stone fences built by the Chinese span miles of countryside in the gold country

1000 men on each side had local blacksmiths making all kinds of spears and knives for the battle that was about to emerge. On October 25, the warriors met in an open field prepared to settle their dispute. The clash took place, but to the surprise of the many spectators who came to see the event, it turned out to be mostly a show of strength instead of an all-out war. In the end about four men had been killed and a dozen wounded. It was recorded as the Tong or Crimea War since it was fought near the Crimea Ranch. Today modern street signs have been placed next to the old stone posts that marked main crossings of this once active little town.

SONORA

This settlement takes its name from miners who came up from Sonora, Mexico. It was also known as the "Queen of the Mother Lode " since it was one of the richest towns in the area. Forty million dollars would eventually be taken in all. One memorable nugget weighed in at 25 pounds! This Latin-influenced community became a dangerous place to live when the "Americans" felt that foreigners should be forced off their claims. The result was a racial conflict where Mexicans and whites in particular raided, robbed and murdered each other. Most everyone wore a gun, and the streets were no longer safe, especially at night. The California government finally passed a law in 1850 called the "Foreign Miners' Tax" that required all non-citizens to pay a $20 fee every month to work their claims. It was intended to drive out foreigners from their rich mines and reduce conflicts. This law was no doubt unpopular among the many miners working the area who were not citizens and many departed. The tax was cancelled a year later with the depletion of the easy gold, and Sonora's violent reputation was soon erased. Since the town was located on a route to Stockton, a supply center, it remained an important transportation link to other mining camps. Even today Sonora continues to thrive as tourists come to visit the lasting reminders of a past time.

SELF-TEST: HORNITOS TO SONORA

1. How did Hornitos get its name? _____
   _____
   a. What did Ghiradelli become famous for in San Francisco? _____
   b. At its peak, how much gold was taken a month from Hornitos? _____
   _____

2. Why was the penalty for stealing a horse often worse than killing another person?
   _____

3. What did Bret Harte do for a living during his stay in La Grange? _____
   a. What was the "Grey Goose?" _____

4. Describe how the "Whistling Billy" got to Coulterville and its purpose: _____
   _____
   _____
   _____
   _____

5. Why were the Chinese persecuted? _____
   _____
   a. What is a tong? _____

6. What was the purpose of the Foreign Miners' Tax? _____
   _____
   _____
   a. Was the tax fair?_____ Why? _____
   _____
   _____
   _____
   _____
   b. Why did Sonora remain an important town after the gold was gone? _____
   _____
   _____

72

COLUMBIA

Our next stop is a place that was discovered by chance. Two brothers, Thaddeus and George Hildreth, happened to be camped here after a period of bad luck searching for gold elsewhere. To make things worse, it rained on them that night. The next morning while drying out, John Walker, another man in the group, did a little panning to pass some time. The date was March 27, 1850. In the two days that followed, the men gathered thirty pounds of nuggets! Soon word spread of a new strike, and the tent town became known as Hildreth Diggin's. It changed again to American Camp, and then finally to Columbia.

It wasn't long until miners discovered they were on top of an ancient stream bed of the Stanislaus River that had long since changed course. The few creeks that drained through the area dried up during the summer months, so two water companies developed a system of ditches and a 60 mile long flume that supplied water to power mining machinery. In a snap, hydraulic and hardrock mining equipment was brought in and began extracting gold at a record rate.

Columbia quickly became one of California's largest settlements. The town included 4 banks, 8 hotels, 2 fire stations, 3 churches, a school, 3 theaters, 53 stores, 40 saloons and gambling places everywhere. Unfortunately, an 1854 fire burned down almost every building in the business district since most were made of wood. The town was rebuilt and the new structures were constructed mainly of brick and stone with metal doors and window coverings to minimize future destruction by fire and for security.

By the 1870's about $87 million in gold had been taken from Columbia; today that amount in our dollars would top $2 billion. But just like other towns that finally gave up most of their gold, Columbia became a ghost town. However, in 1945 the state of California bought many of the old buildings and created a "Living" State Historical Park where men and women dress and play the roles of Gold Rush era personalities. It is the most popular Mother Lode town where more than half a million people visit each year. (See Appendix C, Page 103)

73

CARSON HILL

In 1850, miners struck gold here. In 1851, a 14 pound nugget was dug up. Then three years later the largest mass of gold ever found in California was unearthed weighing in at 195 pounds! It was mixed in quartz and was four feet long, two feet wide and five inches thick. At the time this lump was worth $43,500 at $16 an ounce. In all, about $25 million was taken from the hill, and mining has just recently stopped. In the early days, gold ore was painstakingly chiseled out of deep mine shafts by men using hand tools. Iron carts called "skips" were then each filled with about two tons of the precious cargo as mules slowly struggled along thin metal tracks out to the stamps. In similar mines today, powerful scooping machines shovel blocks of rocky ore into huge dump trucks that sit on wheels eight feet tall. They move about like obedient mechanical dinosaurs and can easily transport one hundred tons of ore at a time to the mill. But unlike mines of yesteryear, tunnels on the most part are a thing of the past. Technology has made it possible to excavate entire mountains of ore resulting in huge open pits. Since a majority of gold taken from contemporary mines can only be seen with a microscope, incredible amounts of ore must be crushed in order to make a profit, and the gold must be chemically removed after being ground powder fine.

"Skips" like this one were once pulled by mules

Giant Electra Haul dump truck taking ore to the mill

MARK TWAIN'S CABIN

This wasn't a town, of course, but the man who wrote The Adventures of Tom Sawyer and Huckleberry Finn caught gold fever himself. He came west in 1861 and mainly supported himself by writing for newspapers. Although he never struck it rich during his wanderings throughout Nevada and California, he did find the inspiration in the Mother Lode to write The Celebrated Jumping Frog of Calaveras County, a very popular tale. The original cabin he rented just outside of Angels Camp burned to the ground some years

Protected remains of the site where Mark Twain lived.

after he left, but it was eventually rebuilt around the original fireplace and chimney. If you use your imagination, you can almost see Twain, whose real name was Samuel Clemens, sitting inside his small cabin behind a table, watching a crackling fire on a cold winter morning, sipping coffee and writing notes for stories. Twain lived here during 1864-65 . . . the final two years of the Civil War.

ANGELS CAMP

George Angel was part of a group that discovered gold at this spot, but Angel found that he could do better selling goods and soon made a fortune supplying miners. For example, when provisions were short a shirt might have gone for $15 and a shovel for as much as $50! These prices would have been outrageous in the eastern states, but no one complained too much, however, because most miners were finding enough gold by 1850 to keep them from going somewhere else to buy cheaper supplies. And leaving a claim would cost them time or maybe even a chance to hit a fortune. Soon the placer gold gave out, and Angels Camp might have become a ghost town if it hadn't been for another merchant by the name of Bennager Raspberry.

Raspberry was known around town because he kept expensive foods for miners who struck it rich. But Bennager was remembered for something more important. As legend has it, he was hunting one day and the ramrod used to load his gun got stuck in the barrel. So he shot into the ground to get it out; and to his surprise, the blast shattered a large piece of gold-bearing quartz rock. In three days that followed he had mined $10,000 and the rush was on again. True or not, hardrock mining kept Angels Camp alive for several more decades.

Today Angels Camp celebrates the Gold Rush days every May which includes a frog jumping contest made popular by a story credited to Mark Twain. The town offers museums and a park dedicated to the miners of the productive Utica Mine. A statue of Twain also stands here commemorating a movie made about him in the 1970's.

(See Appendix D, Page 104)

"Courtesy Levi Strauss & Co., San Francisco."

MURPHYS

Two brothers John and Daniel Murphy founded this town in 1848. They were camped here when they struck it rich panning $400 a day! The Murphys got along well with the local Indians who were happy to trade the gold they found for what they considered more practical items such as blankets. Within a year, the Murphy brothers left, but it should be known that these men were different from most miners – They both left millionaires. Wells Fargo and Co. was quick to build a carrier station as they did in most every boomtown. The glut of raw gold in settlements like this caused the price of the metal to drop, so it could be purchased at a significantly lower price. In addition to transporting gold, occasional passengers and delivering freight and mail throughout California, the company hauled out no less than $15 million in gold from this choice area. The town prospered and many buildings were constructed over the years, including a bowling alley. One of the more famous structures that remains is the Murphys hotel built in 1856. It continues to accommodate visitors today as it did when dusty travelers stepped down from stage-coaches.

STOCKTON

Stockton gained its importance by being situated next to the San Joaquin River which was deep enough for steamships to connect it with San Francisco. This town was a main supply center for miners and merchants in the Sierra foothills. Many trails made their way to and from this busy San Joaquin Valley town, and it remains an active transportation center today.

SELF-TEST: COLUMBIA TO STOCKTON

1. Briefly summarize Columbia's history from 1850 to the present: _____
   _____
   _____
   _____
   _____
   _____
   _____
   _____
   _____

   a. Why were buildings made from brick with metal doors and window coverings?
      _____
      _____
      _____

   b. Explain what had to be done before hydraulic mining could take place:
      _____
      _____
      _____
      _____

   c. By the 1870's how much gold had been taken from Columbia? _____

2. Describe the largest mass of gold ever taken in California: _____
   _____
   _____

3. Compare hardrock mining in its early days to similar mines today: _____
   _____
   _____
   _____
   _____
   _____

4. Name two books Mark Twain (Samuel Clemens) wrote: _____
   _____

continued next page

SUPPLIES PURCHASED IN ANGELS CAMP BEFORE YOU SET OUT TO FIND GOLD:

(Items and prices taken from actual recorded account, 1850)

TOOLS

1 cradle	$18.00
1 pan	2.00
1 dipper	1.25
1 bucket	1.00
2 picks	10.50
1 shovel	11.00

TOTAL $

FOOD

25 lbs flour	$5.00
9 lbs pork	2.70
4 lbs beef	1.20
1 jar pickles	1.00
1 pint molasses	.50
2 lbs sugar	.60
ground coffee	5.00
2 lbs potatoes	.25

TOTAL $

OTHER

1 pair boots	$10.00
2 shirts	5.00
pants	8.25
2 blankets	10.00
canvas tent	30.00
2 candles	.50
1 mule	65.00

TOTAL $

5. What type of mining kept Angels Camp productive for decades? _____

   a. Why did miners pay high prices for the things they needed? _____

   _____

   _____

6. Tell why the Murphy brothers were different from most miners:

   _____

   _____

   a. Why do you think a Wells Fargo bank was built in nearly every rich gold strike

   location? _____

   _____

   _____

   b. Other than gold what else made Murphys a unique town? _____

   _____

   _____

7. Why did many paths lead to Stockton? _____

   _____

   a. What river connected Stockton to San Francisco? _____

MOKELUMNE HILL

This rates as another of the wildest towns in the Mother Lode. Situated on the rising knolls above the river from which the town shares its name, Mokelumne Hill was originally settled by an ex-Colonel of the Mexican War by the name of Jonathan Stevenson. In 1851, several major gold strikes were made in the region, and the town rapidly grew. Two of the larger ethnic groups who settled this area were the French and the Chileans of South America. But with claims staked closely together, it wasn't long before tensions over mining rights increased and many fights occurred in the saloons that stayed open all hours. It was recorded that a killing took place every Friday or Saturday night for 17 weeks in a row! Before long the easiest found gold ran out as it always did; new strikes were made, and Mokelumne Hill was all but abandoned. A town populated by thousands nearly disappeared by the 1860's.

Hand-cut blocks of rhyolite were used to construct this building in Mokelumne Hill

VOLCANO

Established in 1848, Volcano was so named because inquiring prospectors thought (wrongly) that a volcano exploded, and the existing valley was its crater. Unknown to the miners, it was really the eroded bend of an ancient riverbed loaded with rich deposits of gold where hydraulic mining soon effectively removed it.

Another inspiring detail about Volcano is that its early residents seemed to be committed to learning. They set up the state's first lending library, theatre group, literary and debating societies. Nevertheless, within ten years of its rapid start the town began to fizzle out. Many old structures remain standing in this quiet town today, but one of the most interesting is the St. George Hotel because you can still spend the night there.

JACKSON

This place was first named "Botilleas" by Mexican settlers because there was a natural spring where travelers could fill their water bottles. It was later renamed Jackson, probably in honor of Andrew Jackson, our seventh President. Little gold was uncovered until 1856 when Andrew Kennedy discovered a rich quartz vein in the side of a hill. The area turned out to

Kennedy Wheel: Rotating right to left, chambers on the outer ring scooped up waste tailings channeled to it by a flume. As the wheel turned, gravity caused the thick, runny sludge to fall out on the left side to another flume where it was relayed to the next wheel and finally containment dam.

be exceptionally productive where various hardrock mining operations took place until 1942. The yield of Jackson's two most famous mines, the Kennedy and Argonaut, totaled $34 million. The length of one of the many tunnels that sloped into the ground reached nearly 6000 feet.

Jackson has other unique locations worth investigating, too, such as the Kennedy Wheels. Because poisonous chemicals were used in the **cyanide process** to separate gold from crushed quartz, waste tailings became a public safety concern. Loosely controlled, widespread use of these toxins led the government to pass laws in 1912. The new rulings forced mining companies to contain their tailings which helped deter groundwater contamination. Built mainly of wood with metal supports and resembling Ferris wheels, four were constructed to scoop up and elevate mud-like tailings to a holding dam 128 feet uphill from where the gold processing took place. Only two wheels remain intact today, but they are very impressive to see since each one stands 58 feet tall.

SUTTER CREEK

Named after John Sutter who once passed this way, hardrock mining put this town on the map. Placer gold was never very plentiful, but in the surrounding area, which is Amador County today, several deep mine shafts produced gold that was counted in the millions. The streets are still lined with many brick buildings of the late 1800's that show off the wealth of the past. Another lasting feature of the town not to be overlooked is its water-

Items cast at the Kennedy Foundry

powered iron works. Established in 1876, the Kennedy Foundry made fittings used to hold together tunnel supports and parts required for hardrock mines in the area. They still cast specialty items today using methods that have changed very little over the years since its earliest days.

AMADOR CITY

This town emerged as a result of a quartz vein that was interestingly enough discovered by four ministers in 1851. The original settlement was briefly known as Minister's Gulch, but was later changed to its present name after a local rancher who first discovered placer gold in 1848. Five years later the Keystone Mine became the towns most famous producer of gold. At its peak $40,000 a month was taken from the abundantly rich quartz for a total of $24 million. Production stopped in 1912 because of high costs, but was soon reopened until it permanently closed in 1942. The headquarters where Keystone's miners once collected their paychecks has been remodeled as a museum and contains many relics of the past. Also, the rusted **headframe** that raised and lowered workers and ore cars into the mine shaft still exists marking this tunnel's place in history.

Headframe of the abandoned Fremont Mine near Amador City

FIDDLETOWN

The old miners were always complaining that the younger ones were "fiddlin around" all the time, thus the name Fiddletown. Placer gold was first panned in 1849 and settled by people from the state of Missouri. Hydraulic and hardrock mining took place, too, and by the early 1850's several thousand called this camp home including the largest population of Chinese in the gold country. One of the most interesting buildings that remains is the Chew Kee Store which is built of **rammed earth**. At one time, Chinese residents bought everything at this store from specialty foods to herbal remedies to cure illnesses. Few people live here today, and it remains one of the rare places that projects a Gold Rush era feeling.

Chew Kee Store

SELF-TEST: MOKELUMNE HILL TO FIDDLETOWN

1. Name two large ethnic groups who settled in Mokelumne Hill: _____
   _____

   a. What was a main reason fights took place? _____
   _____

2. List three Volcano firsts: _____
   _____

   a. Were all miners who came to California uneducated? Explain your reasoning:
   _____
   _____
   _____

3. What was Jackson's original name, and why was it named this? _____
   _____

   a. Name the two mines where $34 million was taken: _____
   _____

   b. Explain why four huge wheels were built outside of Jackson: _____
   _____
   _____
   _____

4. Why do many of Sutter Creek's buildings remain? _____
   _____

   a. Why was the Kennedy Foundry important to hardrock miners? _____
   _____

5. Why did Keystone's hardrock mining operation stop in 1912? _____
   a. In all, how many years was gold taken from this mine? _____

6. Name three methods of mining that went on in Fiddletown: _____
   _____

   a. Summarize how a rammed earth wall is made: _____
   _____
   _____
   _____

PLACERVILLE

This town had several names throughout its past. Originally known as Dry Diggings because its streams were often waterless in the summer, it was later changed to Hangtown because people there got fed up with law breakers. A person could be accused, tried, convicted and dangling with a noose around his neck in a period of about thirty minutes if he was found guilty. By 1854 this mining camp had progressed quite a bit and several hotels, a theatre and many restaurants were built. As with other early boom towns, gold was plentiful in the surrounding area and many techniques were employed to remove it. And like most rapidly constructed wooden villages, Hangtown was almost completely burned to the ground in 1856 but was rebuilt again with brick and stone. As the town developed into a busy transportation center, its citizens decided to switch its name again to make it sound more inviting to visitors passing through. It was renamed Placerville and has been called that ever since. In its long history many changes have shaped this settlement that separated the Northern and Southern Mother Lode, including transportation and communication technologies. Stage-coaches once passed this way when a suitable trail through the Sierra was opened, and a telegraph line was set up even before Pony Express riders carried news on their way to and from Sacramento. The Central Pacific Railroad laid track in this lively town as well. Today that same route is Highway 50 which is a major road to Lake Tahoe, a popular resort area. Placerville is still a successful community not because of gold, but its location. (See Appendix E, Page 105)

Placerville circa 1855, notice sluice box in foreground   "Kansas State Historical Society"

Cook a famous breakfast, The Hangtown Fry:

1/2 pound bacon
6 to 10 oysters
6 eggs
plain crackers

1/4 cup heavy cream
1/4 cup parmesan cheese (grated)

Fry bacon crisp and set aside. Remove most of the grease from skillet. Dip oysters in 2 beaten eggs, then roll oysters in cracker crumbs. Fry in bacon grease over medium heat, about one minute per side. Beat 4 more eggs with cream, cheese and add anything else you have available that might taste good (that's what they did!) then season with salt and pepper. Pour mixture over oysters in skillet, reduce heat scrambling eggs until cooked. Serves 2 or 3.

COLOMA

This is where it all began. Two men, John Augustus Sutter and James Wilson Marshall, set into motion a chain of events that would cause the world to rush in on California's gold.

Originally from Switzerland, Sutter left his homeland to escape debtor's prison, and in the process left his family who would not reunite with him for many years. Mexico still controlled California when Sutter arrived by way of Hawaii where he convinced government officials in Monterey that he was a war hero and they should let him start a settlement. The officials agreed; the year was 1839 and Sutter, who became a Mexican citizen, had an adobe brick trading post built near the American and Sacramento Rivers with the help of Indian labor. He named his settlement New Helvetia (New Switzerland), and his supply outpost became known as Sutter's Fort.

Years passed and Sutter needed more lumber for his growing demands. He soon hired a carpenter from New Jersey by the name of James Marshall to design a saw mill. It was agreed that it would be built on the south fork of the American River at a valley known by the Native Americans as Coloma. Construction began and while inspecting the **tail-race** that was nearly completed, Marshall noticed something shine in the water.

The year was 1848, probably the morning of January 24. In the days that followed, Marshall curiously delivered what he thought was gold to Sutter's trading fort. They tested the pea shaped nuggets, confirmed it was gold and swore secrecy.

The gold Marshall found on that morning might have been only worth 50 cents, but little did he know that when word got out, and it did almost immediately, he would be credited for opening the world's best-known gold rush—the California Gold Rush!

Almost overnight Coloma became a boom town. In less than a year, the settlement had 13 hotels, 2 banks, countless stores and saloons, tents everywhere, hundreds of claims, outrageous prices for everything and a population of about 10,000. Soon other strikes were discovered throughout the area, and the rush was really on.

Unfortunately for Sutter and Marshall, they never struck it rich. Sutter could not control the flood of people who invaded and took over his property, and he eventually relocated to New York after his outpost was burned to the ground by settlers who disliked him. Add that to poor investments and debts, Sutter died penniless in 1880.

Marshall's end was even more tragic. He never found much gold, so he tried his luck in business, then wine making and failed in both. Finally he went back to what he knew best, the skill of repairing things. He started drinking heavily and eventually ended up in a small town several miles northeast of Coloma named Kelsey. There he owned a small carpenter and blacksmith shop. This is where he also confirmed his reputation as a liar (he claimed to have mystical powers for finding gold), and was little more than a reclusive alcoholic who would sell autographed "Gold Discovery Cards" for a few cents. He died in 1885 the wreckage of his own failures. The citizens of Kelsey did not know what to do with Marshall since he had no family. Due to the summer heat, they put him in a wagon filled with ice and took his body to Coloma. His corpse had lain there for five days before the citizens finally decided to bury him on top of a hill overlooking the river where he had found gold many years earlier.

Five years later in 1890, people started to remember the significance of "Marshall's discovery" and convinced the California Legislature to set aside funds for a monument honoring him. The nine foot statue dedicated above Marshall's grave stands on top a tall concrete foundation but is not made of bronze as it appears. Rather it's a mixture of lead, tin and zinc and painted a bronze color to look expensive. The statue shows the larger than life Marshall looking out over the valley that made him famous but failed to make him rich. In his right hand he grasps a huge nugget (he never found) as a token of his importance. Marshall may not have been a great man in life, but he now stands as a well-known reminder of a past era.

Today Coloma is a 220 acre state park with many interesting sights to see. A replica of the saw mill was built in 1968 but not on the original spot. The first mill was destroyed by vandalism and flooding only two years after its completion. The exact location was rediscovered in 1924, and a marker was erected. **Artifacts** archaeologists uncovered at the site are on display in the park's museum. A person could spend a whole day exploring Coloma, and if the opportunity becomes available a worthwhile visit is recommended.

Marshall Monument, Coloma State Park

AUBURN

Placer gold abounded here in 1848, and it was not unheard of for a man to pan $1500 a day. But... you guessed it, the gold ran out. Auburn might have become a ghost town except that its location made it an important trading center. Many stagecoaches came this way, and the "art" of robbing them began here. The future of the town was assured when Central Pacific Railroad officials decided to lay track through Auburn on their way to Utah. Today houses and businesses in the old section of the city are built on the same hilly streets that miners walked more than 140 years ago.

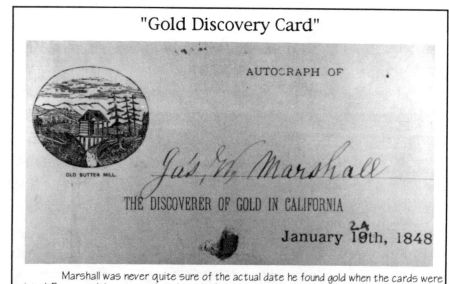

"Gold Discovery Card"

AUTOGRAPH OF

OLD SUTTER MILL

Jas. W. Marshall

THE DISCOVERER OF GOLD IN CALIFORNIA

January 19th, 1848

Marshall was never quite sure of the actual date he found gold when the cards were printed. But a crudely written diary by one of the laborers who helped build the saw mill provided evidence for the most likely date of discovery, and of course Marshall was aware of this correction.

California State Library Archive

SACRAMENTO

This was the site of Sutter's Fort, but its excellent location and overwhelming growth led it to become California's state capitol in 1854. Like other San Joaquin Valley towns, Sacramento earned its importance as a supply center. Situated where the American and Sacramento Rivers join, steamships could navigate all the way from San Francisco. Flooding was a problem, but the city was always rebuilt again. This was considered a "jumping off" point for thousands of gold seekers who came west. Businesses of all kinds were booming, and the streets were overflowing with high priced goods. Try to see Old Sacramento City sometime; it's loaded with a variety of historical sights and high interest museums.

California State Library Archive

GRASS VALLEY

Good Grassland for livestock and timber brought the first settlers to this area around 1848. However, gold made Grass Valley famous in 1850 when a man by the name of George McKnight stubbed his toe on a stone one moonlit night while chasing one of his cows. He brought the sparkling rock back to his house and it turned out to be gold ore! Word of this rich locality quickly spread among miners throughout the region as it rapidly became a boom town.

Hardrock mining became the leading method of extracting gold thanks to the skill of Cornish miners who came from southern England. But mining deep underground was expensive and a large amount of money was needed for equipment. Investors from as far away as London bought in to this profitable venture named the Empire and North-Star Mines. They successfully operated from 1850 to 1956. At its peak eighty stamps milled ore 24 hours a day and eventually yielded over $400 million during that span of time. This was California's richest area.

Most settlements usually faded when the gold disappeared or roads bypassed them, but Grass Valley was one of the few towns that did not meet that fate. It thrived for over a century because of the rich, gold-laden quartz veins that ran for thousands of feet into the earth. Today the two mines are excellent museums well worth visiting.

Just a few miles north of Grass Valley is the town of Nevada City. It is near the site where hydraulic mining was invented by a miner who used a small hand-sewn canvas hose to make his labor easier. His creation was soon developed into huge iron water cannons that introduced yet another facet of mining history.

SELF-TEST: PLACERVILLE TO NEVADA CITY

1. List Placerville's earlier names explaining how each one came about: _____

    _____

    _____

    _____

    _____

    _____

    _____

    a. What destroyed the town in 1856? _____

    b. Name all of the changes in communication and transportation this town has
        seen in its early history: _____

        _____

        _____

        _____

        _____

        _____

        _____

2. What country controlled California when John Sutter arrived? _____

    a. Write a summary for John Sutter and his role in the California Gold Rush:

        _____

        _____

        _____

        _____

        _____

        _____

        _____

        _____

        _____

        _____

        _____

        _____

continued next page

b. Write a summary for James Marshall and his role in the Gold Rush:

_____

_____

_____

_____

_____

_____

_____

_____

_____

_____

_____

_____

_____

c.   Was Marshall a famous person in your opinion? _____ Why? _____

_____

_____

_____

_____

3.   What crime had its beginnings in Auburn? _____

4.   Provide three reasons Sacramento was an important city during the Gold Rush:

_____

_____

a. What natural disaster was a problem for Sacramento in its early days? _____

5.   Why did people first settle in Grass Valley? _____

a. Name the town's two largest hardrock mines and the total amount of gold taken
    from them: _____

_____

6.   What mining technique was invented near Nevada City? _____

MALAKOFF DIGGINS (See Appendix F First, Page 117)

At first you feel like you are on another planet. Yet in the distance you see tall pine trees. From the top, a pit reaches a depth of 600 feet forming a marshy bottom a mile and a half long and over half a mile wide. Yet the rim's sloping walls look like scenery more familiar to a desert. Where are you? Northern California's Malakoff Diggins near the ghost town of North Bloomfield.

California State Library Archive

Hydraulic mining reached its peak in this area and the operation at Malakoff was especially productive. For instance, all the bits of gold collected in just one month during 1882 were melted down to make a block that weighed 510 pounds! Seven monitors worked this pit and the largest could discharge a million gallons of water an hour against the hard-packed sediments they shattered. The power of these cannons was so awesome they could tear a man to pieces if he accidentally stepped in front of one. Until the early 1880's, kerosene lamps lit the night allowing miners to remain active 24 hours a day. Then electric lights replaced them. But this method was very destructive to the environment because of the choking silt and mud that filled rivers like the Yuba, Sacramento and Feather. This practice resulted in mass floods that ruined farmers' fields and drenched the town of Marysville. Glutinous muddy sludge carried by rivers even turned San Francisco Bay brown. Finally in 1884 a California judge handed down America's first environmental judgment: Mining companies could not dump their wastes into streams. Malakoff Diggins soon shut down and the town of North Bloomfield that supplied the men working there was abandoned. Both are museums today, a tribute to the world's largest hydraulic mining operation.

California State Library Archive

OROVILLE

Located near the Feather River, this is where the first successful bucket-line dredge was used to scoop up tons of sand and gravel to extract gold from a river bed. The dredges in this area were big business and operated for more than 65 years. If you have ever noticed uniform piles of gravel along Mother Lode highways that are close to a water source, it was probably the work of a dredge. Oroville is also remembered because the last remaining "wild" Native American came here for help because he was hungry, confused and alone. He was called Ishi and was a member of the Yana tribe. To read more about Ishi, see Appendix G, page 118.

DOWNIEVILLE

It was a difficult trail and 3000 feet of elevation that made Downieville less accessible than most other camps, but those obstacles didn't keep miners away from the rich placer deposits found in the North Yuba River. The settlement enjoyed many prosperous years before fading, but it was another event that made this town somewhat more famous than gold. Around 1851, a hostess of a dance hall named Juanita got into an argument with a miner. He apparently kicked down her establishment's door the previous night when he was drunk. Anyway, sometime during the disagreement she stabbed and killed him. She might have been found innocent; but because the deceased was the friend of many miners, an angry group of vigilantes quickly determined her fate at the end of a rope. She was the first woman to be hung in California. Sadly, vigilante justice was the rule of the day, but fairness under the law did eventually follow.

Northeast of Downieville the Mother Lode extended to its farthest point ending near the supply town of Sierraville. Here the gold country quietly dissolves where the foothills overlook a picturesque valley bordered by the distant jagged peaks of the Sierra high country. Here too, the gold seekers swarmed with the hope that the next mountain or stream held the fortune they came so far to find. Yet for an overwhelming majority, the quest for wealth had eluded them. After months of wandering in all directions from tent camp to boom town, thoughts of ending their search began to linger. Since most found only enough gold to live by hand and mouth and survived in conditions less than comfortable, they simply decided that the best of all possible worlds was at the start of the long journey they had begun — home.

CONCLUSION:

There are many other interesting Gold Rush towns and locations, but the selection briefly covered is very representative of the conditions, events and personalities of this period. California was a magnet for the determined crush of gold seekers who came in force until 1860. And it was only when the news of other rich strikes in Nevada, Colorado, Alaska and North Dakota spread, did the shock waves of excitement echo once again throughout the country. Even so, no other rush in the world would ever match the fury of Californias. In only 25 years beginning in 1849, more than $978 million of the precious metal was taken based on the average of $16 an ounce. Nevertheless, when much of the easy gold had been removed, other kinds of wealth remained. Over the years many towns were built and some disappeared, but most were kept alive by enterprising opportunists who made their living as merchants, farmers or loggers among other professions. It was California's abundant resources, attractive climate, beautiful landscapes and the ambition of many diverse ethnic backgrounds that would shape the state's future.

Nearly all of the towns that came to exist in the beltway of the Mother Lode were staked out because of gold, and along with the arrival of a new population came many ideas and changes both good and bad. On one hand this era saw the rise of transportation, communication and energy technologies that have affected our modern world on the most part for the better. On the other, the Indians' way of life was destroyed and the exploitation or wholesale destruction and misuse of California's resources has damaged its condition. Although the people, land and towns of the Mother Lode have changed as the decades passed, many artifacts symbolizing the Gold Rush have not. Today we can explore the distinctive history of generations before us when we walk among the ruins, buildings and museums that mirror the past. For those who long to see a bygone period, we have the means to experience a time that helps us keep our own values and destinations in focus.

SELF-TEST: MALAKOFF DIGGINS TO DOWNIVILLE

1. Describe the hydraulic mining pit at Malakoff: _____

   _____

   _____

   _____

   a. How many pounds did the largest block of gold taken at Malakoff weigh?_____

   b. What technology made night mining easier during the 1880's?_____

   _____

   c. How many gallons of water could the largest monitor discharge in one hour?

   _____

   d. What town was flooded as a result of hydraulic mining? _____

   e. This town supplied the miners at Malakoff Diggins: _____

2. Name the mining technique that developed near Oroville: _____

   a. Who was Ishi? _____

   _____

3. What is Downieville known for? _____

   _____

   a. Name of the last supply town in the Northern Mother Lode: _____

   b. Do you think vigilante justice was always unfair in the mining camps during the
      Gold Rush? Explain:_____

   _____

   _____

   _____

   _____

   _____

4. Describe what miners did when the easy gold gave out? _____

   _____

   _____

   _____

                          continued next page

5. Looking back on all the towns you read about, describe the kinds of changes that took place in California during the Gold Rush and how they impact us today:

_____

_____

_____

_____

_____

_____

_____

_____

_____

_____

_____

_____

_____

_____

_____

_____

6. Why are historical Gold Rush towns worth preserving? _____

_____

_____

_____

_____

_____

_____

_____

_____

_____

_____

_____

EXAMPLES OF REPORTED GOLD FOUND IN CALIFORNIA

Source	Year	Amount	
Carson Hill	**1854**	**195**	**pounds**
Monumental mine, Downieville District	1869	1893	ounces
Monumental mine, Downieville District	**1860**	**1596**	**ounces**
Knapp's Ranch, Columbia District	1850	50	pounds
French Ravine, Sierra County	**1855**	**532**	**ounces**
French Ravine, Sierra County	1851	426	ounces
Pilot Hill, El Dorado County	**1867**	**426**	**ounces**
Sullivan Creek, Columbia District	1849	408	ounces
Gold Hill, Columbia District.	**1850**	**360**	**ounces**
Holden Chispa nugget, Sonora District	1850	25	pounds
Mokelumne River	**1848**	**25**	**pounds**
Downieville	1850	25	pounds
Fricot nugget, Spanish Dry Diggings, Auburn District (crystallized gold)	**1865**	**201**	**ounces**

*SELF-TEST

WORK SPACE

1. How many ounces of gold were taken from the Monumental Mine in 1869? _____

2. In what area was the most gold found?
   _____

3. Name the mine that produced 30 Troy pounds in 1850:
   _____

4. What kind of gold was found at Spanish Dry Diggings? _____

5. Find the difference between the largest and smallest amounts of gold on this chart:
   _____

6. Find the total amount of gold at all locations to the nearest Troy pound: _____

*Use Troy measurement to answer the following questions. Troy weight is measured 12 ounces to the pound and is commonly used to weigh precious metals.

ARCHAEOLOGY: THE LOST GOLD SHIP
CENTRAL AMERICA

"The ship immediately after, at 8 o'clock on Saturday evening, sank, going down at an angle of 45 degrees, stern foremost. The suction of the ship drew the passengers under water for some distance, and threw them in a mass together. When they reached the surface the struggle for life was intense, with cries and shrieks for help, especially from those unable to swim"...Thomas W. Badger, survivor.

The SS Central America, 272 feet long   "Courtesy of the Mariner's Museum, Newport News, Virginia"

In 1985 modern technology made possible the location and eventual recovery of America's most valuable shipwreck lost at sea. Aboard a well equipped research vessel, an ambitious exploration team known as the Columbus-America Discovery Group set out to find the SS Central America that had disappeared in 1857. The exact location of the ship was unknown, so using the only information available, newspaper accounts of survivors, the team isolated a likely but massive 1400 square mile area off the coast of South Carolina. Hoping their research would pay off, they began to methodically scan the Atlantic Ocean using high-tech computers and sonar equipment that detects objects on the sea floor. Applying this system the team was able to chart images for later investigation. But their task was incredibly difficult as well as time consuming because of the vast territory and great depths they searched.

Three years of ceaseless probing, patience and nearly $10 million in expenses eventually paid off as these modern day gold seekers chose to examine an image they discovered years earlier. The team sent down their specialized box-like salvage robot christened "Nemo" to inspect the subject. One and a half hours later and nearly 8000 feet below their efforts would be rewarded. Nemo's cameras cast light upon the wreckage of a wooden paddle wheel that turned out to be the remains of the hoped-for Central America. After sinking on a return trip from Panama more than a 130 years ago, members in the control room witnessed the video images of hundreds of rare coins, gold bars and everyday life artifacts valued today at over $400 million. The once vanished steamship would not be forgotten.

The Central America was a luxury side-wheel steamer that regularly transported mail, travelers and California gold brought to the Atlantic side across Panama's isthmus. On board its final voyage were about 580 passengers and crew including many who were returning from the gold fields with their personal fortunes. Guarded below deck were three tons of gold in various forms destined for banks.

On their way to New York, the Central America's Captain made a scheduled stop under the blue skies of Havana, Cuba unaware that bad weather was approaching. Unknown to anyone, this would be the large, powerful ship's last fateful portage. As they pressed on toward the east coast, a severe storm rolled in across the Atlantic. Huge waves and high winds tossed the steamship about and its stressed hull began to leak. The coal got wet, and its 750 ton engines were unable to generate power. The water pumps then failed, and despite the passengers best efforts to remove water in a bucket line relay, the boat slowly sank. A nearby ship bravely helped recover women and children as the storm raged on, but for many this was their last voyage —fewer than 160 would be saved. On Saturday September 12th just after 8 PM, the huge steamer already sunk to deck level, lurched and began a long descent toward the ocean floor. Terrified men were forced to throw off their money belts filled heavy with gold and jump into the violent foaming waves that crashed in the darkness. Many were pulled down in the vacuum created behind the doomed ship as it plunged into the deep. On the surface, a confusion of debris and pitiful cries filled the expanse of turbulent water; a majority would not survive the night slipping into the cold, voiceless depths of the sea forever.

In their last hours all the gold in the world was worthless to the Central America's abandoned passengers. Nothing could save them from an inescapable tragedy that abruptly shattered their lives in a horrifying moment of reality. For us, however, an instant of history and wealth was frozen in time. Because of technology and a determined exploration team, lost treasure and priceless artifacts will find their way into museums for us to appreciate. The remains of an untouched moment have been preserved, capturing a bygone century that shaped the events all of us share today.

SELF-TEST

1. How were the explorers able to locate and recover the Central America's treasure?

   _____

   _____

   _____

2. What kinds of information do you think can be learned from the wreck?

   _____

   _____

   _____

   _____

   _____

3. Why do you think the Central America is important today? _____

   _____

   _____

   _____

   _____

IMPORTANT DATES OF THE CALIFORNIA GOLD RUSH

After reading through these important dates, answer the questions on the following page:

1775-80   Discovery of gold by Mexican miners in Southern California.

1842   Gold discovered north of Los Angeles on the ranch of Francisco Lopez.

1848   James Marshall discovers gold on the American River, triggering a major rush.

1849   Quartz mining began at Mariposa. The first stamp mill in the state was probably used here.

1850   Gold ore was found in Grass Valley. This led to the development of underground mines that lasted for over 100 years.

1852   Hydraulic mining begins just north of Nevada City.

1854   A 195 pound mass of gold, the largest known to be found in the state, was found at Carson Hill.

1855   The bulk of easy placer gold was largely exhausted by this date, but other methods of mining requiring machinery had taken over.

1857   The side-wheel steamship Central America sinks in a storm off the coast of South Carolina taking with it many lives and three tons of gold thought lost forever.

1864   Hydraulic and hardrock mining had taken over as the chief gold production methods. By this time the main part of California's Gold Rush had ended. Other rich mineral strikes throughout the nation were being made.

1880   Hydraulic mining reached its peak in the state. Systems of reservoirs, tunnels, ditches and flumes supplied water to the operations. These same water systems would also be used to power electric generators providing inexpensive energy to Mother Lode towns.

1884   Judge Lorenzo Sawyer issued an order making it illegal to dump tailings into the Sacramento and San Joaquin Rivers and their tributaries. This meant the end of hydraulic mining.

1895   The cyanide process of extracting gold from crushed ore was first introduced at the mines of Bodie, CA on the eastern side of the Sierra near Mono Lake. This made it possible to recover of 95% of the minerals locked inside ore.

1898   The first successful steam powered bucket-line dredge was used on the Feather River near Oroville. Gold dredging soon became a major industry.

1922   The Argonaut Mine Disaster. A fire on the 3350-foot level of the Argonaut Mine near Jackson caused the loss of 47 lives.

1933-35   The price of gold increased from $20.50 to $35 per ounce. This resulted in more exploration and greater production of gold in the state.

continued next page

1942   World War II causes a drop in gold production. Congress issues Order L-208 on Oct 8, forcing all gold operations to close because they made use of explosives and iron—materials critical for weapons production.

1946   Order L-208 was lifted July 1. Some dredging resumed, but only a few important hardrock mines such as the Empire and North-Star Mines in Grass Valley reopened.

1956   The Empire and North-Star Mines in Grass Valley closed down for good. Rising costs and the low price of gold ended this most productive operation.

1965   Governor Edmund Brown signed Bill 265 making gold California's official state mineral.

1968   The last gold dredge working near Oroville was shut down October 1.

1989   The Columbus-America Discovery Group begins recovery of three tons of gold that went down with the steamship Central America. This was made possible because of modern technology.

SELF-TEST

1. By what year had the prime of the Gold Rush ended? _____

2. In 1898, what type of mining was becoming a major industry? _____

3. What did Order L-208 do? _____

4. Why was the cyanide process important to miners? _____

_____

5. What caused more exploration for gold in 1933-35? _____

_____

6. How many men died in the Argonaut disaster of 1922? _____

7. Why were many Gold Rush towns ready for electrical generators when they became available? _____

_____

8. Copy the blank time line guide below on a separate piece of paper and place the events for questions 1 through 7 in the order they occurred. Expand your time line if you choose by adding extra entries from pages 1, 96 and 97.

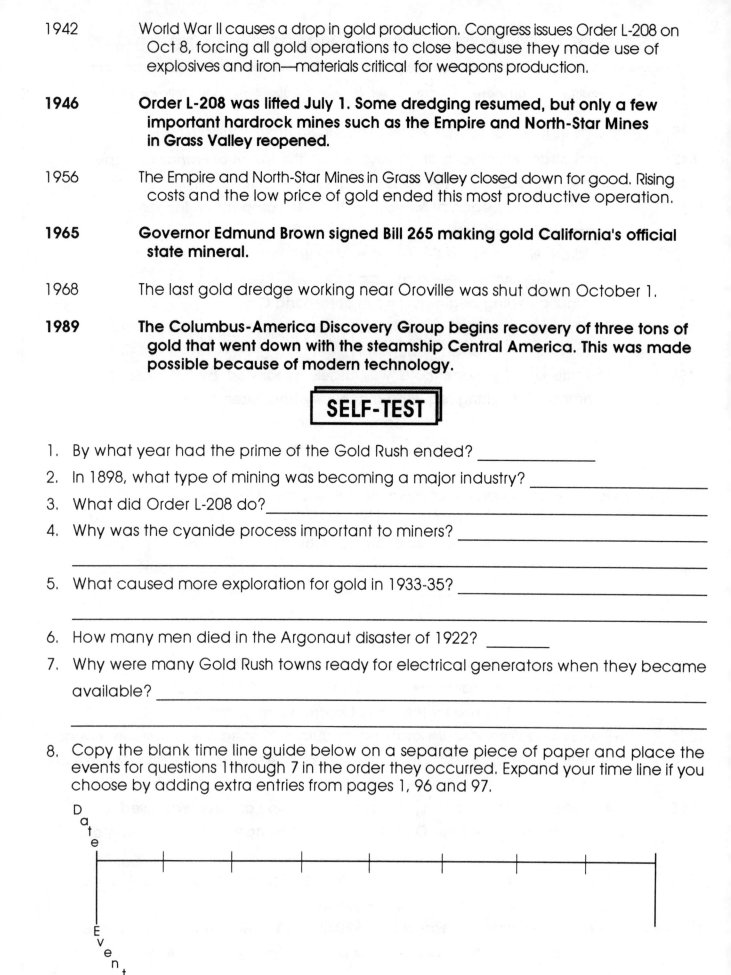

VALUE OF GOLD IN THE 1980'S

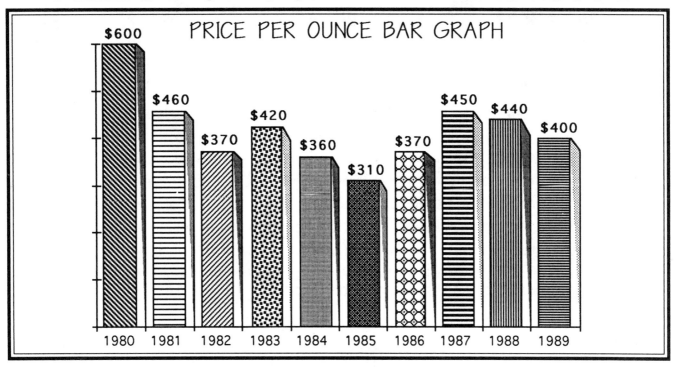

PRICE PER OUNCE BAR GRAPH

$600 — 1980
$460 — 1981
$370 — 1982
$420 — 1983
$360 — 1984
$310 — 1985
$370 — 1986
$450 — 1987
$440 — 1988
$400 — 1989

SELF-TEST

After examining the chart of gold prices for the 1980's answer the following:

1. What year was an ounce of gold worth the most? _____

2. Which years was the price the same? _____and_____

3. Find the difference in value between the highest and lowest years: _____

4. What was the best year to buy gold to make the most profit if you sold 100 ounces in

   1987? _____ What is the total profit you would have made? _____

5. Find the average price of gold for the '80's:_____ (Hint: add values for all ten years then divide by 10)

6. Is the answer to number five higher or lower than the price today? _____
   (The current price of gold can be located in newspapers, TV business news and coin shops)

   A. What is the difference? _____ B. What do you think causes this difference?

   _____

   _____

WORK SPACE

JOSEPH GOLDSBOROUGH BRUFF, 49ER

Bruff worked as a map maker for the government in Washington D.C. and was the seasoned age of forty-six years old when he left for California in 1849. Serving as captain for the sizable Washington City Company he, unlike most travelers, wrote vivid journals and drew illustrative sketches of his adventurous undertaking. Little escaped his watchful eye as he recorded the variable weather conditions and landscapes, breakdowns of wagons, fallen animals and the many graves he encountered along the way. He also noted the friendships, generosity, suffering and cruelties he observed during his trek to the gold fields in revealing detail.

Well into their journey west, Bruff's company left the Humbolt River electing to take the Applegate-Lassen Cutoff. It turned out to be a poor choice where even the last 35 miles through the Sierra to Lassen's Ranch proved to be tough. Mules and oxen dropped dead from exhaustion; wagon wheels, axles and hitches snapped on the rocks and trees that bordered the steep demanding narrow trail. Without remaining spare parts nor animals, wagons were abandoned. Bundles of shovels, books and every imaginable kind of belongings carried thus far were thrown out along the trail or sometimes even buried with the hope of returning to collect them later.

It was during this final push in late September that Bruff's own company faced the loss of so many animals that some of their wagons had to be given up. Bruff alone agreed to stay with the possessions they were forced to desert, so they would not be scavenged by passing argonauts. He did this with the understanding that someone would come back for him with fresh livestock as soon as possible. Unfortunately for Bruff no one would return. While he diligently guarded supplies that would never be reclaimed, he filled his time by drawing and writing as he waited, offering coffee and conversation to the hardened, ragged travelers who briefly visited his camp.

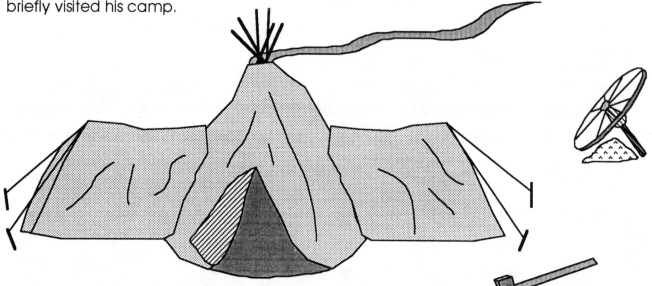

Bruff constructed a crude shelter very similar to this drawing. It was made from wagon covers and had a fire pit in the center. Unlike this illustration, it was surrounded by tall pine trees and since it was next to the trail, the ground was littered with a variety of items disposed of by earlier companies.

(continued next page)

Weeks passed, winter snows arrived and Bruff was sealed in the mountains with his food supply soon gone. The few others who were trapped with him were forced to eat whatever they could find to survive. The following selection is what Bruff recorded in his diary on Sunday December 23, 1849 as they searched through deep snow for an ox that had died of exhaustion in early November:

"...We went to search for the ox carcass, within 50 yards of the (tent), which 6 weeks ago I had complained of as (odorous). We found a large stump, (and) beside it lay the ox (we found) by probing with an iron rod. We dug away the snow and soon exposed him; and with an ax, cut off the fore leg, at the knee-joint; then cut around the shoulder with a butcher knife, and dragged it to our lodge. We cut the meat into pieces, boiled them, added salt, pepper, water and a handful of moss from an oak; stewed nearly dry, and with coffee once more filled our stomachs. This meat, when raw, was of a light lead color, blotched with reddish spots. We could detect no unpleasant taste, — if any taste at all. Had a sound night's (sleep), and our health extraordinary under such circumstances."

Eventually Bruff was reduced to eating coffee grinds to keep his pains of hunger away. But at his first opportunity in early spring, he hiked out from his deadly situation to Lassen's Ranch where he was able to recover from his ordeal.

He began his search for gold without much luck; and after considerable travels throughout California he returned home by way of the Panama route in 1851. Bruff intended to publish his journals and sketches, but the technology of producing complicated drawings inexpensively simply wasn't available. He died in 1889 never realizing his ambition. It would not be until 1944 that his work was first published capturing one of the best detailed records that has preserved the images of a true 49er.

WHAT DID THE MINERS DO FOR ENTERTAINMENT?

Unfortunately, the earliest miners who arrived in California didn't have much to do in their spare time. Between the hard work and endless search for gold, all were faced with the difficult task of amusing themselves the best they could. Some fell into a routine of drinking, gambling and losing what little savings they collected. Most miners did gamble and drink at least once in a while, but many also passed away their idle hours writing letters home; the most time consuming part of which was finding someone to deliver them! Some played music, sang songs or danced while others just slept. Miners had to be especially creative during the winter months when they were confined to their tents or cabins. If it was too cold to work a claim, good conversation about family or future plans while smoking their pipes and drinking coffee around a fireplace must have been constant pastimes.

Few families were in the mining camps at first, so during pauses between gold fields bored miners could always find a table where they played various card games such as Monte, Faro, or a Chinese game called Fan Tan. Yet another popular entertainment was bear and bull fights. In this unusual contest, a bear was trapped and sometimes chained to a stake in the center of a small make-shift arena. A bull was then released into the ring; its freedom and gouging horns were considered an even match to the slashing claws and power of the bear. Bets were placed among the shouting men as the terrified animals were cruelly forced to fight until one died. Strange as it may seem to us, these battles were big events and a favorite with many miners far away from home looking for excitement and diversion.

In the coming years, more civilized entertainments such as traveling theatre groups, singers, dancers and even lending libraries soon helped entertain the miners, who once parted with their earnings in less traditional ways. And with the arrival of more women, many men began to take on the responsibility of "settling down" and establishing the foundations of family life.

101

(continued next page)

HOW TO PLAY THE GAME OF FAN TAN

Fan Tan is one of the many games that miners played to socialize or pass away the long hours of boredom they endured. This is a game that the Chinese brought to America, but of course anyone with money could participate.

Chinese coin used in Fan Tan. Actual size shown
Notice the square hole cut in the center

Markings indicate the 4th emperor of the Qing Dynasty and was minted between 1735-1796(author's collection)

To play, all you need is a pile of pennies (The Chinese used their own copper coins since they were considered useless in the mining camps), a bowl and, for our use, play money.

Start by taking a handful of pennies and slap them down on a table as you quickly cover them with the bowl. Remove any coins sticking outside the bowl's rim. Now everyone places a bet on odd, even, or the exact number of hidden coins. After all bets are made, the dealer uncovers the coins and stacks the pennies in piles of four. If there are one or three left over, those betting "odd" double their money. If none or two are left, the "even" bets win. Those who guessed the exact total triple their bets.

If a miner won, he still had to pay a percentage of his winnings to the dealer. It's easy to understand why these gambling houses never went out of business. And in our present time it's not too hard to figure out who pays for the casinos in Reno or Las Vegas!

SELF-TEST

1. Name four things miners did in their spare time:

    A) _____ B) _____ C) _____ D) _____

2. Why do you think gambling and drinking were common?_____

    _____

    _____

3. Other than what has been mentioned, make up two things you might have done for entertainment if you had lived during the Gold Rush: _____

    _____

    _____

    _____

    _____

    _____

COLUMBIA'S VIGILANTE JUSTICE

By the middle 1850's a system of courts had been established throughout the Mother Lode, but **vigilante justice** was still a strong force in some areas. One such example had to do with a man named John Smith who had been drinking when he walked into Martha Carlos Barclay's Long Tom Saloon on October 10, 1855. He seemed to be looking for a fight, and when he broke a beer pitcher Martha ordered him to leave, but Smith refused and pushed her down into a chair. Just at that moment Martha's husband John Barclay walked in and saw what looked like Smith's hands around his wife's neck. Without hesitating, Barclay pulled out his gun and shot Smith dead.

During this period of history, an accused person might only have to tell the sheriff what happened and would most likely have been found not guilty during the trial. But two things were working against John Barclay. He was a new member of the community, and the man he shot was a close friend of California Senator James Coffroth who just happened to be there at the time. Coffroth was a convincing speaker and soon had a crowd ready to hang Barclay on the spot. A "court" was quickly put together, but the jury already knew what their answer would be...Guilty! The sheriff at last arrived and tried to protect Barclay, but the unruly crowd knocked the lawman unconscious and forcibly took their victim.

A rope was thrown over a 30-foot high flume and a noose pulled tight around his neck. With the help of about a dozen men, Barclay was pulled into the air, but in their hurry they forgot to tie his hands. He struggled to keep the rope from choking him to death. Finally, someone climbed up the flume and pried his hands loose. The lynching was complete, but more trouble was to follow. The angry crowd returned to the Long Tom Saloon and smashed everything, and they didn't stop there. They continued to vandalize and loot the entire main street district wrecking a tremendous amount of property.

The next morning many of the town's citizens were shocked at the news from the day before. Even so, this would not be the last time vigilante justice would take place in other untamed Mother Lode towns.

LEVI'S

The pants we have all come to think of as "Levi's" had their beginnings during the Gold Rush. Like many others, Levi Strauss, originally from Germany, came to California in 1853 to earn his fortune. However, he planned to sell dry goods in the boom town of San Francisco rather than shovel earth in search of gold. Upon arrival, Strauss used his business mind to fill a need by making pants from canvas used for tents, ship sails and wagon covers. The only problem was that miners seemed to rip out just about any kind of sewn material quickly because they were always filling their pockets with heavy rock samples or tools. In 1872 Levi met Jacob W. Davis a tailor from Carson City, Nevada who used copper rivets to strengthen his pockets together at stress points. Word about Davis' "wear-like-iron" pants spread, and Levi quickly convinced him to run his shop. The two men patented the use of rivets the following year, thus "Levi's" were born.

A more popular material was eventually used by Strauss in the production of his pants. A cloth originally from Genoa, Italy had spread throughout Europe. This "Genoese" fabric was eventually shortened to "jeans," and so the name. The durable cloth was soon produced by the French which was made from cotton and dyed with the blue color of the indigo plant; they called it denim. Levi's denim "blue jeans" became very popular with the miners and held a reputation for quality. Strauss even claimed in advertisements that horses could not pull apart a pair of what he liked to call his "waist-high overalls." The loose-fitting jeans he manufactured had button flies, suspender buttons instead of belt loops and did not look as trim as they do today, but miners were more interested in a pair of long-lasting work pants, not style.

SELF-TEST

1. Who first used copper rivets to hold pants together? _____

2. What is denim? _____

_____

3. How did the word "bluejeans" come into use? _____

_____

_____

4. Describe an early pair of Levis: _____

_____

_____

_____

☞ CHARLES BROWN: DIARY OF A GOLD SEEKER ☞

He was just twenty-four years old and struck with gold fever in the spring of 1850. Originally born in Pennsylvania, Charles Brown migrated to Iowa in 1844 attracted by the rich agricultural lands of this prime Midwestern state. In addition to farming, Brown eventually established a successful tavern that proudly displayed his name and comforted overnight travelers. Since his business was near the Mormon Trail, one of the routes that led west to the gold fields, he was no stranger to the passer-bys who undoubtedly shared their knowledge about California gold.

Even though he was aware of the stories and wealth promised by the gold fields in 1849, he was not quick to jump on the bandwagon. He had a family, crops to tend and a business to run. It's easy to imagine Charles with his family and relatives sitting around the dinner table discussing the latest news of the rush and the magnetic attraction it had upon the scores of people who were making their way west. There's little doubt that Charles thought he, too, could quickly find a fortune in California and return home the following year to help with spring planting. He certainly must have been thinking of what arrangements could be made to have his family provided for while he was away sifting through California's golden rivers.

As with many others, Charles was caught up in the moment of a historical event that seemed like a fool's journey to some. But how could anyone be sure? There was just too much excitement in the air for all talk of easy gold to be rumors. It took about a year, but he finally convinced his family that the journey was worth it. He took care of the responsibilities that kept him home and made preparations to cross the unspoiled continent.

Like most gold seekers in 1850, Brown didn't get an early start because of the unusually wet spring. On May 8th, he set out for California from his Tavern with an unnamed Iowa company and a jumble of friends or acquaintances some of who left before, some after his departure. Charles elected to take his horse and shared a wagon loaded with what was reasoned to be enough food and supplies for the long journey.

Brown's fragmented company traveled very loosely as they caught up with or passed each other at various points along the trail. Despite their lack of organization, they felt secure in the numbers of similar adventurers going in the same direction, and it seemed a remote possibility that hospitality of some kind would not be extended if the need arose.

Since Brown traveled in a small group he reached Council Bluffs, Iowa near Omaha on the eastern edge of Nebraska's border in good time. Beyond this landmark they followed the Platte River occasionally joining other sizable companies but never staying with them very long as they were able to move faster. Having chosen the Mormon Route, which paralleled just north of the Oregon-California Trail, the company followed the Platte to the Sweetwater River whose source laid at the base of the Rockies. When Brown's party was well into the rugged passes of this mountain system, they chose a cutoff that led them into Nevada's Humbolt River Basin. While larger, better equipped companies slowly struggled along, Brown's smaller group readily passed them. However, his lack of an adequate food supply was becoming apparent. And when it ran out he was quick to discover that many argonauts were increasingly possessive about their foodstuffs and did not part with them easily. He became dependent upon the generosity of others, and had to pay high prices for something as basic as flour—*if* it could be obtained. Little relief of any kind was available and only sheer determination to reach the California gold fields set the standard for Brown to continue.

Aware that the Applegate-Lassen Cutoff was not the best route to take, they continued to follow the Humbolt. At Big Meadow (more commonly referred to as Great Meadow) near the end of the river, Brown gave his horse to a company that agreed to board him and a friend for the remainder of the trip. As the Humbolt finally gave out it formed a shallow marsh-like lake or "sink" filled with abundant grasses where companies rested before continuing. Upon leaving, Brown's group chose the Mormon-Carson Route where they endured a forty mile stretch of nearly waterless desert filled with the casualties of hardship. When they reached the eastern side of the Sierra, Brown crossed the mountains south of Lake Tahoe where he descended into the heart of the gold country at Placerville exhausted and grateful the journey was over. After five months of travel, and seeing the continent as none of us ever will, Charles soon began working claims he staked along various streams in the Mother Lode and slowly collected what was to him a small fortune.

*Throughout his journey Brown kept a reasonably accurate diary of his adventure. He seemed confused about distances at times, but without accurate maps it's very understandable. His bare bones entries are written in a very simple, direct style that recreates his unique view of the time. While other diarists complained bitterly of their difficulties, Brown's strong character led him to omit such accounts of these same hardships. He certainly must have been touched by the scores of dead animals he encountered each day because a separate record of these was kept. Nevertheless, he reveals little overall emotion of his experience but does provide an interesting day by day journal that helps us see into his window of the past.

*What follows is a transcript of Brown's 1850 diary. Except for obvious misspellings or interjections for clarity, no changes have been made.

MAY

8th   First day very muddy. Stayed near Sacks

9th   Next very muddy. Stayed near Bermingham

10th   Roads better. Stayed near Squire Pings

11th   Roads quite good. Got a letter at Agency City from *Joseph Sprott dated May the 3rd. Stayed at Colwells on the Demoines River and laid up half the day.

12th   Crossed the Demoines River. Camped on Millers Creek.

13th   Wrote a letter home mailed at Albia Monroe Co. Camped on Cedar Creek. Found J. Sprott inscribed on a tree dated May the sixth, also grass plenty.

14th   Left Cedar this morning struck the Mormon Trace (trail) from Edyville to Chariton Point. Found paria (prairie?) very extensive. Roads very dry. Cattles' feet appear sorethis evening. Camped on prairie 2 miles from timber in Lucas County, Iowa.

15th   Fine morning. Cattle appear lively. Struck the main Mormon Trace at Chariton's Point by noon. Camped 10 miles west of Chariton.

16th   Pleasant morning. Roads fine. **Joseph Hendricks over took us 15 miles west of Chariton Point. We passed a grave on the north side of the road with the following words at the head: E.B.W. who accidentally shot himself on 13 of May 1850 aged 22 years. Camped on Camp Creek.

17th   On the night of the 16th our cattle run off. Found them next evening 8 miles north. Left Camp Creek at sundown. Traveled 10 miles. Camped near White Brest. Timber.

18th   Left early and crossed Grand River at Mt. Pisga at 4 o'clock. Mt. Pisga is situated on the east side of Grand River 200 miles from Keokuk (Iowa) and (is) a very rough and poor place. Camped on the west side of Grand River in Company with 23 teams.

19th   Sunday morning started early. Left our company behind. Crossed second prong of Grand River this morning at 8 o'clock. Crossed a small creek at noon (and) struck in a prairie 25 miles (across). Camped in prairie. Commenced raining at sun down.

20th   Rained until 10 o'clock. Crossed a small creek at 3 o'clock and camped on the west side of Notaway (?) Creek with 18 (other) wagons. Left the Company.

21st   Early next morning traveled 3 miles. Over took Abraham Sorter and Co. McCrady crossed a creek at noon. Crossed another at 4 o'clock. Camped with A. Sorter, C. McCrady and Barney of Keokuk and Doctor Dressor of Nashville (Lee County, Iowa).

*Joseph Sprott was a part of Brown's company who had set out several days earlier.
**J. Hendricks was yet another part of Brown's loosely formed company

MAY

22nd   Crossed east nation (established states?) at 9 o'clock. Camped on a small creek. Commenced raining at sundown (and) continued next day until noon.

23rd   Cross the west nation (new U.S. Territory?) at 4 o'clock. Camped on the west side and caught fish.

24th   Crossed Silver Creek at 10 o'clock. Camped 5 miles of Kanesville (Iowa).

25th   Arrived in Kanesville 10 o'clock, wrote two letters home. Camped 6 miles above town at the foot of Council Bluff (near Omaha, Nebraska). I am on top of the bluff. It is quite a curiosity. It is 3 hundred feet high and as far as I can see East, North or South, there is nothing to be seen but sharp peaks like great mounds, and at the foot of the hill there is a fine spring. It is one mile to the Missouri River across a fine prairie.

26th   Crossed the Missouri River at 12 o'clock in camp 3 miles west of the river in company of Wheelock's teams.

27th   Pleasant morning. Some appearance of rain. Left the American Eagle Company. Commenced raining at 10 o'clock. Passed another Company. Mr. C. McCready and Robinson left us. Crossed the Horn (River) at sun down, in camp near Horn.

28th   Traveled 12 miles across the bottom and struck the Platte (River) Camped with the Independent Mining Co.

29th   Joined the Independent Mining Company in command of Hiram Tyrrell of Illinois. We had a Pawnee Chief with us last night, had some difficulty with the Pawnee Indians. Two of the men left the train, and one had his shirt taken off his back, and one his pistol and the Indians had taken up the bridge (crossing). There was some 60 with their chief. Had to treat with them before we could pass.

30th   Traveled up the Platte. Camped on a small lake in company with 32 wagons near the Loop Fork.

31st   Crossed the Loop Fork 3 miles from the mouth. Camped on the west side one mile from the ferry. Mr. Barney shot a deer.

JUNE

1st   This morning I am sitting on the west bank of the Loop Fork of Platte herding cattle. Traveled up the Loop Fork (and) saw a great many deer elk and antelope. Camped on the Loop in company with 32 wagons.

2nd   Sunday morning had a shower of rain. Last night clear and pleasant. This morning left the Independent Mining Company. Traveled with the Nelson's Company of 8 wagons. Camped on the Loop with a Horse Company.

JUNE

3rd   Traveled with Barney and Sorter, struck across the Platte. Camped on the divide and had a very hard rain.

4th   This divide is very sandy. Sharp peaks. Scarce any grass on the hills, and out of sight of timber. Passed a wagon that had been left, and a buffalo that had been killed this spring. There was an antelope killed today. Barney and I were out this afternoon, saw two, shot at one but did not get it. Crossed Prairie Creek this evening. Rained all night.

5th   Rained until noon. Crossed Wood Creek (and) encamped on the Platte.

6th   Barney and I left the train this morning for a hunt. Went across the bottom 4 miles to Word River. Traveled up the river, saw a great many antelope, and on my return I saw Wheelock after a buffalo on his horse. I lit off (shot at), Jim shot at it (and on his horse) run it 3 miles to Wood River (and) shot it while swimming across, in the jaw, and while going up the bank (on the other side) shot it in the leg. It limped off and lay down. Went back to the train. Simon A. Sorter and John went back, swam across but could not catch it. Encamped near Grand Island.

7th   Traveled up the Platte in sight of teams on the south side of the Platte.

8th   Passed 8 graves in the last 3 days and passed through many "dog towns". They are a small animal the size of a squirrel. (i.e., Prairie Dogs)

9th   Traveled up the Platte, passed the Iowa Will Company of 18 teams. The night of the 8th their cattle got scared and run over the wagon guard, and killed one ox. 25 of their cattle are gone yet. They (stampeded) and run for miles with the wagons. Encamped near a grave also one at (noon). I . Ward and E.G. Hagard (names on grave markers).

10th/11th   Traveled up the Platte river. We find grass plenty and have ever since we crossed the Missouri. River water and timber for cooking but for nothing else. Barney shot a deer at noon. I went out and carried it on my horse. Camped near the last timber on the north side of the Platte.

12th   Passed two graves this morning. Passed a great many dead buffalo. Encamped on Bluff Creek near the Sandy Bluffs and near the Platte.

13th   Raining this morning, and I am 4 miles up Bluff Creek on the bluff a looking at miles. Hederick (Hendricks?) a running 12 buffalo. We have had very sandy roads all day. Encamped on the Platte.

14th   Pleasant morning, nooned on the Platte. Barney and I went out a hunting. I shot a deer and carried it 4 miles before me on Jim (before Jim arrived?) to the wagon. Encamped on the Platte, have good grass.

JUNE

15th   Passed one grave at noon. Encamped on the Platte. Teams on the other side of the river.

16th   Passed two graves today. Camped on the river bank. 3 encampments on this side of the river, and 4 on the opposite in sight.

17th   Monday had sandy road. Encamped near Ancient Bluff Ruins on high clay banks, a few rock and cedar (around).

18th   *Encamped in 6 miles of Chimney Rock. It is on the opposite side of the river. It is a high peak with a rock on top 10 feet in diameter and 40 feet high.

19th
and   One of our ox's feet is wore out, and we drive with the three yoke. One of Barney's also. Encamped on the river. Lay up half the day and left our stove my trunk.

20th   Encamped 4 miles above Scotts Bluff on Spring Creek, saw some Indians. We are 476 miles from (Brown's Tavern).

21st   I am on Spring Creek a herding cattle this morning. The water (is) very clear and cold, and the mosquitoes are as thick as I ever seen.

22nd   Encamped on the Platte. Grass very scarce.

23rd   Arrived at the ferry this morning near the fort (Laramie). The fort is between the Platte and Laramie fork. In the forks of the river I wrote a letter home and bought nails for shoeing oxen for $6.25 for a hundred nails. Encamped three miles above the ferry on the north side of the Platte. Joseph Sprott is one day ahead of us.

24th   Shod one of our oxen with leather. Traveled with 4 yoke. Had a very hilly rough road. Encamped near the river. Plenty of timber, pine cedar and cottonwood and good grass.

25th   Very good roads but hilly. Encamped near a Mr. William's grave who died June the 25th of cholera.

26th   Nooned on the Platte opposite Laramie Peak. We have seen it for the last 6 days. It is very high, some 20 miles from here. Encamped on the river.

27th/28th   Crossed over the Black Hill. Encamped near the river. I went on ahead (to camp) with J.W. Sprott on the Platte 80 miles from the fort. Overtook Sprott, Wheelock and Lauman at noon. Crossed big hill. Encamped on the Platte, grass short.

*From six miles away Chimney Rock certainly did appear very small to Brown. It is actually a sandstone column nearly 500 feet high where hundreds of gold seekers scratched in their names in the soft stone. Weathering has since removed all markings.

JUNE

29th   Road very hilly and sandy. Nooned on the Platte. Encamped on the Platte in 4 miles of the upper ferry. Grass very scarce. Watched our cattle on the sand bluff all night.

30th   Passed the ferry early this morning, ascended a hill 7 miles long and nooned without grass. Traveled until night and no grass. Went until 10 o'clock, tied up our cattle without grass. Traveled 30 miles.

JULY

1st   Find ourselves surrounded with camps. Hunted until 10 o'clock for grass, (and) found. It is three miles from the camp, and have lay up for the day. Joseph Sprott and I are a herding at the present time, also Scott and A. Sorter left early this morning.

2nd   Passed 2 graves. Had very sandy roads and no grass. Encamped on Sweet - water (River). It is 75 miles back to the ferry and nothing but wild sage and very hard, sandy roads.

3rd   Traveled 2 miles and camped for grass near Independence Rock. When on the summit we are in sight of snow to the southwest and to the north and east we are in sight of large lakes of pure *saleratus. Passed one grave and came in company with John D. Plotts Company of the Prairie Rivers (wagon) No. 2.

4th   I lay out all night last night 7 miles from the camp. Sweetwater grass has been good. Encamped 17 miles from Independence Rock. Passed 3 graves.

5th   Traveled 18 miles, passed 2 graves. Encamped on Sweetwater. Grass scarce. Snow in sight.

6th   Crossed Sweetwater 3 times in one mile and traveled 7 miles and encamped for grass. Passed 2 graves. I was attacked with a violent fever.

7th   Left Sweetwater and traveled over 16 1/2 miles of sandy desert, and crossed Sweetwater and encamped on the bank of the river. Passed one grave.

8th   Traveled 17 over sage plains and encamped on Sweetwater.

9th   We find some ice this morning, also we passed a snow drift 8 feet deep. Fremont's Peak 15 miles north of here is white with snow. Traveled but 10 miles. Camped on Sweetwater.

10th   Traveled 15 miles over the summit of the **dividing ridge or the South Pass. Encamped on Pacific Creek. Very cold and snow in every direction. Passed 5 graves.

* Refers to a chalky looking, baking soda color. This was due to the high concentrations of alkali in the lakes.
** His reference to the "dividing ridge" or South Pass is the Continental Divide.

JULY

11th   Left Pacific Springs and traveled 23 miles and encamped on Little Sandy (creek). Passed 7 graves.

12th   Left Little Sandy and trailed over to Big Sandy (creek) 12 miles. Passed 5 graves. 13 dead cattle.

13th   Lay all day recruiting our teams. Sent our cattle 8 miles to graze.

14th   Lay by until 3 1/2 o'clock P.M. and then started across the desert of 45 miles. Traveled all night, passed 2 graves that we knew of.

15th   Daylight still found us traveling on the desert and very dusty. Arrived at Green River at 4 o'clock P.M. Passed 3 graves. Ferried Green River and encamped on the west side and sent our cattle 6 miles to graze.

16th   Lay by all day to recruit our cattle.

17th   Started out and traveled 15 miles and encamped on a branch of Green River on good grass, but some alkali. Passed 12 graves.

18th   Traveled 18 miles over lofty mountains and encamped on a branch of Bear River. Here we meet plenty of Indians of the Snake tribe. They appear friendly. Passed 6 graves. Drove our cattle 1 mile to graze.

19th   Lay by all day to recruit our teams.

20th   Started and traveled on and nooned at a stream 2 *rods wide, then climbed a very high mountain. When on the summit, we got a refreshing shower of rain. Encamped on the mountain after a travel of 15 miles. Passed 8 graves. Took our (cattle) 1/2 mile to graze.

21st   Still in the mountains. Arrived at Bear Valley (Wyoming) at 2 o'clock P.M. after traveling 19 miles and passed 10 graves. Drove our cattle 3/4 mile to graze.

22nd   Traveled 12 miles down Bear River (and) got a heavy rain. Encamped about 3 o'clock. Passed 6 graves and drove our cattle 1 mile to graze.

23rd   Traveled 19 mile in forepart of the day. We passed over some of the highest mountains yet, but continued for 6 miles. Balance of the road good. Passed 3 graves. Took our cattle 1 mile to graze.

24th   Traveled 8 miles down Bear River, and encamped on a small branch and lay 1/2 the day. Good grazing up to the wagon. Passed 1 grave.

* 1 rod equals 16.5 feet

JULY

25th   Traveled 20 miles on Bear River and encamped at Cedar Spring. Took our cattle 1/2 mile to graze. Passed 2 graves.

26th   Passed the Soda Spring and Steamboat Spring and nooned at the forks of the Oregon Road and Greenwood's Cutoff. Left Bear River and took the Cutoff. Went 8 miles and encamped at the foot of the mountains. Took our cattle 2 miles to graze.

27th   Traveled 15 miles over mountains and encamped on Reed Creek. Sent our cattle 1 mile to graze. Passed 4 graves.

28th   Traveled 6 miles. Nooned at a creek. Encamped at the foot of (a) mountain, no water, 1 grave.

29th   Crossed the mountain and lay up for the day. C. McCrady over took us. Took our cattle 2 miles to graze, passed 4 graves.

30th   Traveled 15 miles and encamped 2 miles (into) the 25 miles desert. Pass 2 graves.

31st   Traveled 23 miles and encamped on a small spring branch. 2 graves.

AUGUST

1st   Traveled 20 miles. Find plenty of water and grass, 4 graves.

2nd   Traveled 20 miles. Encamped in a valley in sight of Humbolt Mountain. 2 graves.

3rd   Struck the mountain in 8 miles. Traveled up a creek 8 miles encamped. Good grass. Passed 4 graves, also struck the Fort Hall Road at the creek by noon.

4th   Traveled 16 miles, plenty of water and grass. Encamped in 1 mile of Salt Lake (City) Road. Passed 7 graves.

5th   Traveled 17 miles over very bad roads and encamped on Goose Creek. Passed 5 graves.

6th   Traveled 8 miles and encamped. Found our breadstuff short. Killed one of the oxen and jerked (salted and dried) the meat, and divided it amongst the Company.

7th   12 miles. I have been a hurting for provisions all day. Offer 50 cents a pound for flour and can not get any. Have made up my mind to go a bed and pack.

AUGUST

8th This morning Simon Martin and I have everything ready to start. Lauman Sprout and Barney give us bread to start on forward, will was good, but he had none to spare. Larabee (member of his Company?) was a little selfish. Traveled 13 miles and come to a spring. Grass scarce. Struck Cold Spring Valley. Grass more plenty. Had a very cold rain. Encamped in the valley. Lay on the cold ground. Passed 6 graves, D.K. Bower (name on grave marker?).

9th Traveled on roads very dusty. I bought 2 pounds of flour for 2 dollars. Encamped within split log (location?). Michael (member of his Company?) was treated very kindly to a good warm supper and breakfast. 5 graves.

10th Start early, very warm and roads dusty. We passed a mountain on the left. Noon at a good spring. The mountain(s) south of us are covered with snow. I find that we are traveling down (the) *Mary's River. This afternoon encamped at the crossing of a creek with Mr. Ricky. Bought bread (from) him for supper and breakfast. Passed 6 graves, traveled 30.

11th Traveled down the river. Noon(ed) on the river this afternoon. Roads dusty. Pass over some hills, cross a creek, and in camp in 3 miles with North's Company. 35 (miles) Passed 9 graves.

12th Start our early travel down the river. Noon(ed) where the river join(s) up to the bluff. The river is some 4 rods wide here, and there has been very good grass ever since we struck the valley. Seen Samuel Dalzell. Crossed the river 4 times and camped in 2 (miles) of the canyon. Passed 4 graves.

13th Start early, nooned on the mountain at a spring, struck the river and crossed. Traveled down some 8 miles and encamped with a Missouri train. Passed 2 graves and one man lying at the side of the road dead.

14th Start out. A great talk of Indians. Travel 2 miles saw a wagon left stating (message attached to wagon?) that a man was killed the day before and cattle stolen. Nooned in 5 miles after crossing a hill. Travel 18 miles over a sage plain, and camped on a river with a Missouri train. **There was 21 cattle stolen from the Iowa train, and 40 men went out well armed to get the cattle. Run the Indians in a canyon in the mountain, and exchange(d) a few shots with them and left without the cattle. They are a bidding $2 a pound for flour.

15th Start out early, traveled 12 miles and noon(ed). It is very warm and dusty. The dust is ankle deep. Travel down the river and camp with 2 Missouri teams.

16th Travel 9 miles to a hill. Cross over and noon on the B (backside). Travel over a second hill and travel down the R (river), and camp with 3 wagons from Wisconsin. Got some meal and a pound of coffee. 3 graves.

*Same as Humbolt River
**Digger Indians lived along the Humbolt and occasionally took unguarded cattle for food.

AUGUST

17th   Travel down the (Humbolt) river 33 miles and camp with mule teams.

18th   Start early, travel 15 and noon. Travel 12 mile, very sandy roads. Struck a sage plain 13 across. Travel until 10 o'clock at night. Had nothing but a plate of beans for supper. Spread our blankets on the ground and lay until morning.

19th   Bought 2 pounds of rice and a small piece of bread for $1.50, also 2 quarts of meal for $1. Nooned on the river making one stop before the Indians would not let us. Travel down the river 10 miles and camped. Drove my horse across the river to graze.

20th   Cool morning. Waded the river for my horse. Travel down the river 25 miles to the Big Meadow (Also known Great Meadow). Find plenty of grass.

21st   Travel 10 miles without anything to eat. Can not buy (food) at any price. Come across Mr. Wilson from Henry County, Missouri. Give him my horse to board Mr. Simon and me to the mines. *Travel 15 miles and camp on the lake.

22nd   Start out early and travel down the lake 9 miles and leave for the desert. I was taken with colic and sick all day and night (yesterday and last night?). This morning at day light finds us on the desert. I am some better. It is **3 miles to the river. There is a great amount of destruction amongst the wagons, horses and cattle. I counted in the last three miles 175 head of cattle, mule and horses (dead), and it has been the same all through the desert.

23rd   We arrive at the Salmon Trout River (same as Truckee River) by 9 o'clock. Find a great many traders here. Flour $2 per pound, pies $1.50, a piece of beef 30 and 50 (cents), a pound of bacon $1, for one meal $2.50. Water on the desert 50 cents a gallon. We met with the two Mr. Dungans here. They start out this evening for the mines with their pack(s) on their back(s).

24th   Traveled 6 miles and stopped to graze on the river.

25th   Traveled 14 miles over the sage plain and camped on the river (This was most likely the Carson River also called the Pilot River at the time). Good grass.

26th   Traveled 12 miles across a sandy plain and nooned on the river. 6 miles and camped on the river.

27th   Traveled 1 mile and crossed the river. 17 miles and crossed back and camped.

28th   Leave the river, travel 12 miles over stony road, and return to the river again and noon. Leave the river, 6 miles of sandy road, and two miles down, good grass.

*As the Humbolt neared its end in the desert, it took the form of a marsh-like lake.
**This is after traveling many miles over a stretch of desert with only one poor quality spring along the way.

AUGUST

29th   Traveled 18 miles up the Carson Valley and camped near the mountains. Good grass.

30th   Traveled 16 miles along the foot of the mountains and camped near the canyon.

31st   Traveled 8 miles up the canyon, found very rough roads. The worst I ever saw.

SEPTEMBER

1st   This morning we are surrounded by high mountains, the tops covered with snow. We find plenty of frost this morning. We have been traveling near and through pine for the last three days. Traveled 10 miles and nooned near a lake. 5 miles over the worst mountain I ever saw through heavy timber. In camp with 50 teams. The pine is very high and large.

2nd   This morning we struck the Sierra Nevada Mountains. Find it very steep and rough, and near the top the wagon hubs drag in snow. And when we were on top we had a snow storm. Traveled 12 miles.

3rd   Traveled 15 miles and camped at the Leek Springs. (Bought) groceries here. Call it 50 miles to Hangtown (Placerville).

4th   Teams lay up to recruit. Simon and I take up some provisions, and strike out for Hangtown. Travel this afternoon 25 miles and kindled our fire and lay out tonight in the mountain(s).

5th   Start early 25 miles to town got (in) at noon.

SUMMARY: Left Hangtown September 22, 1850 for Kelsey's Diggins. Rain commenced on November 20. Left Louis Town the 10th of January (1851) for the Middle Fork of the American River. Left Oregon Bay the 23 of April, camped on the Middle Fork of the Yuba near the mouth of Wolf Creek. May 4 through Onion Valley, snowed all day. Crossed snow 10 feet (deep). Camped on the South Yuba. Near Bridgeport, Nevada County (California). Left Bridgeport. Oct the 9th left the American River the 12th. Took the stage at Auburn the 13th for Sacramento City. Took the steamer the same day at 2 o'clock for San Francisco. Land at 9 o'clock the same night.

CONCLUSION: Charles spent about ten months in California wandering about searching for gold. When he possessed $1360 from his efforts, he set out for home leaving San Francisco on October 14th aboard the steamship *North America*. Arriving on the Pacific side of *Nicaragua, he traversed the country's jungle trails and crossed its central lake by canoe to the Atlantic side. Upon reaching the eastern edge of the continent on November 4th, he was able to buy passage aboard the ship *Brother Jonathan* and landed in New York on the 28th. Making his way to Philadelphia, Pennsylvania, probably by stagecoach, he soon arrived in Pittsburgh on December 5th. From there he traveled to Cincinnati, Ohio, which put him within a few days of his family and home in Iowa.

*In addition to the Panama crossing, Nicaragua was also a favored way to return from California by sea during 1850-52.

WILLIAM SWAIN, GOLD IN CALIFORNIA

William Swain was one of the original 49ers. Like many, he left his family and farm with high expectations to seek a fortune in California, but in the end failed to accomplish it. What Swain did find was an incredibly difficult passage crossing the varied geography of the American continent. And even though he began with a large, well-equipped company of 61 men and 18 wagons, hardship and tempers caused the group to break up in the Sierra. Swain entered the gold fields only with what he could carry on his back, but he managed to keep the diary of his experiences leaving for us an accurate account of what it was like to live and travel to California during the Gold Rush.

He began his search for gold on the Yuba River just outside Malakoff Diggins long before hydraulic mining was introduced to the area. He spent about a year prospecting without much luck before facing the hard truth that he was not going to get rich. Discouraged, he returned home by sea not wanting to make the strenuous journey by land again. Within weeks, Swain was reunited with his family in New York bringing back little gold but many rich memories. Here is a firsthand account of a letter he sent to his wife during his stay in California:

"Many persons are returning home, tired of California....That there is an immense amount of gold here none can deny, but it is much more difficult to obtain than it was last season....In short, the cream has been taken off....

You will ask, what is the average amount daily made by the miners? This much is quite certain, that...every miner who has at least some experience expects to make an ounce a day, or else he is not satisfied with his placer and will prospect for a better one. Often we hear of men making an average for several days from $50 to $300 per day; in fact, there is no doubt but such is the case. Many have certainly through the past year made from $5000 to $10,000....It must be understood that not all make this money by digging. Most of those who have done so well are those who brought capital with them and went directly to trading in the mines or in the city of San Francisco or Sacramento and other places. This gave them very great advantages, as everything sold at enormous profits."

Born in 1822, Swain lived to be 83, and the record he kept is a valuable insight to a powerful experience.

Q. How old was Swain when he ventured to California? _____

Ishi, The Last Yahi

In August 1911 an Indian appeared at a slaughter house near Oroville. He seemed to be starving, confused and was wearing a ragged canvas shirt that reached to his knees. He looked to be about 45 years old and was speaking an unusual language. No one knew what to do with him so he was taken to the Oroville jail to let the sheriff decide. In the meantime, word spread of a "wildman" who survived even though all the Indians in the area were thought to be gone. Soon, newspapers all over the state were being filled with stories of a "stone-age man."

The news quickly reached San Francisco and University of California Professor Thomas Waterman who became interested in the reports of the man who spoke a language no one understood. He had studied the tribes that once lived in the area, so he telegraphed the sheriff and took a train to Oroville the same day to see the mysterious captive.

Upon meeting the Native American who spoke no English, the Professor began to repeat a list of words he brought from various tribes of the area in an attempt to communicate with the frightened man. Finally, Waterman struggled to pronounce a word that was understood. He was shocked to realize that he was speaking to a member of the Yahi tribe, a group that lived in the foothill canyons east of the Sacramento River thought to be wiped out. Excited at the chance to learn about a little known culture, Waterman made arrangements with the sheriff to take charge of the stranger whom he called "Ishi," which means "man" in the Yahi language.

It turned out that Ishi was the last of his tribe. He was the final link of a culture thought to have been destroyed by the many invaders gold had lured to California. When miners flocked to the Mother Lode foothills in 1849, they brought with them diseases such as chickenpox, smallpox and measles. These illnesses silently killed Yahi and other tribes by the hundreds. Conflicts between the Indians and Whites resulted in even more deaths and the eventual destruction of the Yahi. Only Ishi had escaped illness and detection until hunger and loneliness drove him from his home.

Ishi was introduced to a new world. He received a job at the university museum, and over the years he learned many English words while at the same time teaching his own language and culture to the Professor. During the remainder of his life, Ishi demonstrated many skills he used when he lived among his people. But in March 1916, disease ultimately took Ishi's life forever ending a way of life this world will never see again.

Interested in Ishi?   Good books to read are: **Ishi Last Of His Tribe** or **Ishi In Two Worlds** , both by Theodora Kroeber

GLOSSARY OF TERMS

ARTIFACTS: Any object made or shaped by humans.

ALKALI(ZED):   Natural concentrations of salts and mineral oxides that makes water bitter tasting. Drinking heavy concentrations can cause illness or poisoning.

AMALGAM: Combination of gold and mercury locked together that can only be separated by heat or acid.

ARGONAUT: An adventurer by land or sea.

ASSAYER: Individual who tests the purity of minerals and determines their value.

BUFFALO CHIPS: Dried buffalo droppings that can be burned for fuel.

CHOLERA: An intestinal disease caused by bacteria that spreads easily through food, water, or bodily fluids and is very deadly if untreated.

CYANIDE PROCESS: Method developed by German chemists using a mixture of water, the poisonous chemical cyanide (that liquefies gold) and zinc shavings (to capture the dissolved solution). This made possible the recovery of 95% of all minerals locked inside ore that was crushed powder fine. Many tailings were profitably reworked as result of this discovery.

EMIGRANT: Person who travels from one location or country to another.

ETHNIC GROUP: Race of people linked by a common language, beliefs, foods and artifacts.

FLUME: Sloping trough usually made of wood used to conveniently transport water over long distances.

FOUNDRY: A business that casts objects made from metal.

HARDROCK MINING:
      Type of mining where gold-rich quartz veins are picked and blasted apart. This creates deep mine shafts or open pits, and the ore must be crushed to extract the gold.

HEADFRAME: Structure erected over the top of a mine shaft that supported cables fed out from a hoist. Miners, ore carts and equipment could then be safely lowered on steep tracks that led underground.

ISTHMUS: Narrow strip of land that connects two larger masses. The country of Panama is one such example.

MALARIA: Type of disease transmitted by mosquitoes in tropical regions causing high fever and eventual death without treatment.

MERCURY: A heavy silver-colored liquid metal that can be used to bond with gold particles.

MOTHER LODE: The rich mineral beltway through California located roughly from Mariposa north to Downieville and known for its rich gold deposits.

ORE: Rock containing gold or other minerals.

PLACER GOLD: Loose, free gold that has been eroded from its original source.

QUARTZ: Generally a white-colored rock where many gold deposits originally formed. Most is hidden underground, but some "veins" reach the surface and are known as outcroppings.

RAMMED EARTH: A Chinese method of constructing walls for buildings by mixing together clay, sand and limestone with very little water. The prepared mixture was packed inside a temporary hollow wooden frame and pounded with metal rods from the top until solidly compacted. These highly durable insulating walls were formed in six to nine feet sections and were about two feet thick.

SCURVY: Caused by lack of vitamin C obtained from fruits and vegetables. This disease triggers swelling of the gums, bleeding under the skin and general weakness resulting in death if untreated.

TAILINGS: Waste rock left over from various mining techniques.

TAIL-RACE: A U-shaped open ditch diverted from a river used to control the flow of water that turned a water wheel. After powering the wheel, the water continued in the channel back to the river.

TECHNOLOGY: Inventions created to make our lives easier or better.

TRANSCONTINENTAL:
To cross or connect a continent. Highways, railroads an electronic communications are examples of how a continent can be linked.

VIGILANTE JUSTICE:
A group or committee of citizens who administer justice in order to immediately judge and punish an individual for a suspected crime.

Index

Bibliography (selected)

Wagner, Jack R. Gold Mines of California.
Howell-North Books, San Diego, CA

Warren L. Hanna. Lost Harbor.
University of California Press, Berkeley, CA

James P. Delgado. To California By Sea.
University of South Carolina Press.

Hunt, Thomas H. Ghost Trails To California.
Nevada Publications, Las Vegas, NV

Judy Conrad and Barry Schatz. Story Of An American Tragedy. Columbus-America Discovery Group, Columbus, OH

Alistair Cook. Alistair Cook's America.
Alfred A. Knopf Inc., NY

J.S. Holiday. The World Rushed In.
Simon and Schuster Publishers, NY

J.B. Bruff. James Goldsborough Bruff.
Columbia University Press, NY

Don and Betty Martin. The Best Of The Gold Country.
Pine Cone Press, Walnut Creek, CA

Nigey Lennon. Mark Twain In California.
Chronicle Books.

D.B. Wilson. A Mysterious Chapter in the life of John A. Sutter. California Historical Society Quarterly (Dec 1959). San Francisco, CA

Rowe Findley. The Pony Express: Grit and Glory.
National Geographic Society (Jul. 1980), Washington D.C.

Harold Curran. Fearful Crossing. Nevada Publications, Las Vegas, NV

Delores J. Cabezut-Ortiz. Merced County: The Golden Harvest. Windsor Publications Inc.

Theodora Kroeber. Ishi In Two Worlds.
University of California Press.

Erwin G. Gudde. California Gold Camps.
University of California Press.

Smithsonian Exposition Books. The Smithsonian Book of Invention. W.W. Norton and Co., NY

Carman, Kimmel and Walker. Historic Currents in Changing America. The John C. Winston Company, Philadelphia.

Phil Ault. Wires West. Dodd, Mead and Co., NY

ORDER FORM
(Please Print Clearly)

Name or Organization:_____

Address:_____Apt # _____

City:_____State:_____ Zip:_____

Please send _____Copy(s) at $14.95 each (CA residents please add 7.25% ($1.08) sales tax)

Answer Key for Self-Tests available for an additional $6.95

Shipping: $2.00 first book, 75¢ each additional and Self-Test Answer Key

Send check or money order to:
FreeWheel Publications
California Gold Rush
PO Box   3853
Merced, CA 95344

☎ (209) 726-8441

THANKS FOR YOUR ORDER!
(allow 2-4 weeks for delivery)

Copy(s) $14.95 x _____ = $	
Answer Key $6.95 = $	
Shipping = $	
Tax (CA) = $	
TOTAL = $	

Free Self-Test Answer Key with orders of 35 or more books!

Printed in the United States of America